Dear Hannah,

Enjoy!

Love,

Grandma & Grandpa J.

Saddle Pals

*Memories of favorite horses
shared by readers of Country and
Farm & Ranch Living.*

*S*addle *P*als

Publisher: Roy J. Reiman
Editor: Jerry Wiebel
Associate Editors: Paula Wiebel, Mike Beno
Art Director: Bonnie Ziolecki
Art Associates: Ellen Lloyd, Claudia Wardius
Photo Coordinators: Trudi Bellin,
Mary Ann Koebernik

© 2000 Reiman Publications, LLC
5400 S. 60th St., Greendale WI 53129

Country Books

International Standard Book Number: 0-89821-266-9
Library of Congress Catalog Card Number: 99-75107

Front cover photo: Jack Westhead
Pages 3, 5 and back cover photos: Christopher Marona

For additional copies of this book or information on other books,
write: Country Books, P.O. Box 990, Greendale WI 53129,
call toll-free 1-800/558-1013 to order with a credit card or
visit our Web site at **www.reimanpub.com**.

Horse Lovers Share Stories From the Heart

By Jerry Wiebel, Editor

CHERYL LEFLAR had a special bond with her horse and faithful companion Whiskey.

I f you love horses, this book will bring a smile to your face on one page…and put a lump in your throat on the next. That's because the readers of *Country*, *Country EXTRA* and *Farm & Ranch Living* who contributed to it spoke from the heart as they shared memories of their favorite horses.

These readers and their horses were more than saddle pals. By reading their letters, it was easy to see there was a special bond between them that allowed them to move as one as they galloped down a country lane.

As that bond grew stronger, they even thought alike and understood each other's emotions. When one made a mistake, the other was ready to forgive. They were friends in the truest sense of the word.

On horseback, these readers could dream of being anything they wanted to be—cowboys, trick riders, knights in shining armor and beautiful princesses. As they rode down the trail, they left their troubles and cares in the dust behind them.

Cheryl Leflar of Fort Collins, Colorado explained it best as she told about her first horse, "Whiskey".

"There are so many great horses in the world that never receive the recognition they deserve," she writes. "They may not be world-class champions or famous racehorses. But they are every bit as special to those humans who love them and share that short but sweet piece of life that God grants us."

Horse lovers can appreciate how much Cheryl wanted a horse. "When I was young, I not only dreamed about owning a horse someday, I used to pretend I actually *was* a horse most of the time! I never wore out the seat of my pants, just the knees. I often asked Mom to feed me my cereal (grain) in a bowl on the floor so I could eat just like a horse!"

Cheryl eventually got her wish. "Whiskey was a golden Palomino gelding of questionable parentage," she continues, "but no one ever questioned the size of his heart.

"He would stand quietly for hours while I bathed, combed, braided and fussed over him. That same carefully tended mane also soaked up many of my tears when, as a teenager, I believed he was the only friend I had."

Cheryl tells of riding Whiskey in the Colorado mountains. "He never faltered in carrying me wherever I wanted to go,"

"*S*ome horses may not be champions, but they're every bit as special to the people who love them…"

---

she relates. "No trail was too difficult to deter his brave heart, and I felt safe with him underneath me."

Eventually Whiskey went blind, and Cheryl could no longer ride him. "I found an even greater peace just being with him, though, brushing the flies from his cloudy eyes and whispering my dreams to the one who always seemed to have time to listen," she recalls.

"The day I had to put him to sleep was the hardest of my life. My friend had gone to a better place and left me behind with only my memories.

"I know Whiskey is romping in Heaven now, his head held high and his eyes clear. God has promised us all green pastures, and no one deserves them more than he does.

"Save one more ride for me, old friend."

Saddle Pals is chock-full of stories like this one…of ponies that carried youngsters through childhood…magnificent mounts that pranced in parades…and hardworking stock horses that didn't quit until the ranch chores were done.

So saddle up and join us for an enjoyable trail ride down memory lane.   ∩

She Kept God Awake All Night Praying for a Horse

By GeNeil Avery, Tuscaloosa, Alabama

My Prince Charming came into my life when I was almost 10 years old. He had eyes that looked like large pools of chocolate, red and white hair and four legs. You see, my first love was a horse!

A horse of my own seemed like an impossible dream because we lived in the middle of Memphis, Tennessee. But my dad understood this dream. When he grew up on his folks' farm, he, too, wanted a horse of his very own and eventually got a big beautiful white one.

So one summer day in 1937, Mom and Dad approached me with a plan. If we could sell the puppies my terrier, "Rags", had delivered a few weeks earlier, and if we could get permission from the Board of Health to keep a horse in the garage in our backyard, then they'd see about making my dream come true. A few weeks later, the puppies were all gone and permission came from the Board of Health.

We set out the next Saturday to look at ponies advertised in the newspaper. There were several to look at, and I probably could have settled for any of them—that is, until I met "Prince".

Fell Hopelessly in Love

Prince was grazing in the far corner of his yard. When we appeared, he stood still as a statue, head up, nostrils flared, eyes unblinking as he looked us over. Then, quietly and elegantly, he walked up to me, nuzzled my cheek and put his soft nose in my outstretched hand. I fell hopelessly in love.

Unfortunately, Prince's owner was asking $15 more than Dad could afford to pay. That night as I lay in bed, I heard him and Mom discussing the money problem.

I decided to take this situation to a higher authority and went straight to God. I think I prayed most of the night. God and I got very little shut-eye!

Sunday after church, my aunt came along as we went back for another look at Prince. The owner must have realized Prince and I were meant for each other, because she dropped the asking price $10. My aunt chipped in the extra $5, and Prince was mine!

I still remember the way Prince softly nickered when I went out to feed him each day, brushing his fine coat until it would shine like a copper penny, smelling the fresh cedar shavings Dad unloaded in the stall and going for long rides—just Prince and me.

Sometimes Rags would get in on the fun, too. When I saddled up to go riding, she'd come running and jump as high as she could right next to my stirrup. I'd reach down and try to grab her. It would take several tries, but she never gave up. When we connected, I'd put her up in front of me and we would ride down the streets of Memphis.

Dad passed his love of horses on to me...and when I married, moved to a small ranch in Texas and had two sons, I passed this love on to them. They got their first pony for Christmas the year they turned 6 and 7.

As far as I'm concerned, everyone ought to have a Prince (or Princess) Charming in his or her life at least once.   ⌒

GENEIL AVERY sits atop Prince clutching her terrier, Rags. Her father is pictured below on his big white horse in 1912.

9

'Grandpa' Pepped Up
Before the Big Race

By Kathryn Leeman-Smith, Aurora, Colorado

My favorite horse memories are from the year I was a 13-year-old Girl Scout in Las Vegas, Nevada. My troop took riding lessons every week for a year from Edna Gray. She was in her 60s, and she was tough, but fair.

Edna owned a stable full of horses. Some we loved, others we dreaded. She taught us to saddle, bridle, curry and feed them all.

"Raspberry" was a beautiful roan, but very skittish and hard to control. "Queenie" and "Bell" were huge draft horses. We would walk bowlegged after riding them bareback. "Popcorn" was white with speckles. He had eye trouble, and

> "No one wanted to ride Grandpa. I could crawl faster than he wanted to walk…"

we always had to let him know well in advance of our arrival.

There was one horse we dreaded—"Grandpa Blue". When he was much younger, his coat was so black that it almost looked blue. That's how he got the name Blue. But by the time we met him 29 years later, Edna had added Grandpa to his name. We thought it should have been "Slowpoke", "Pokey" or "Dead" instead!

He Moved in Slow Motion

None of us wanted to ride him because he was so slow on trail rides. I could crawl faster than he wanted to walk. He did everything in slow motion. He would even fall asleep before we finished brushing him.

Then came the day of our graduation and rodeo. We were all excited until we discovered that Grandpa Blue was one of the horses in the rodeo.

Everyone had to draw the name of a horse out of the hat. I drew Popcorn for my mount in the rodeo. He wasn't my first choice, but at least he wasn't Grandpa Blue.

Then my best friend drew. I knew she picked Grandpa Blue when she burst into tears. I felt so bad for her that I offered to trade, but Edna wouldn't let me. She just kept saying, "You'll be surprised."

We showed our skills in several events. Then it was time for the barrel race. I thought I did pretty well until Grandpa Blue took his turn. It was as if someone had given him a bottle of pep pills and lit his tail on fire. He came in first place!

We figured Grandpa Blue was an old rodeo horse, and he got excited and his adrenaline started flowing when he entered the arena. But when I saw him later at summer camp, he was back in slow motion again. ○

Jean Higgins/Unicorn Stock Photos

She Wanted a Paint Like Little Joe's

By Julia Farnham, San Marcos, California

I had fallen in love with Paint horses when I was a little girl watching Little Joe on the television show *Bonanza*. So when I was 19 years old and working on a ranch, I became determined to get a Paint of my own. However, Paints were becoming very popular, and their prices were way out of my price range.

The ranch manager and I finally found a registered Paint broodmare in foal that was for sale. He agreed to buy the mare and I'd buy the foal when it was born. At the last minute, the owner decided not to sell the mare—but after a little persuasion, he agreed to still sell me the foal.

Several months later, I got a call that the mare had given birth to the prettiest filly she'd ever produced. I bought her sight unseen, which was a crazy thing to do, and after she was weaned, she became mine. The filly's registered name was "Puddins Patches". She had almost identical markings on each side of her body, and I thought she was the most beautiful horse in the world. What a gift from God!

Acted Like a Puppy

Patches had the most loving and gentle disposition. I started taking her for walks when she was 6 months old. I didn't even have to keep a lead rope on her—she followed me around like a puppy.

As a yearling, Patches liked to play with my dog. She noticed that when I whistled, my dog would come running to me and receive lots of loving. Pretty soon she was racing the dog whenever I whistled to get a hug, too. Sometimes she'd cheat and try to nip at the dog so she could get the loving first.

When she was 2-1/2 years old, it was finally time to ride Patches. After months of groundwork, the moment I had

> *"If I tried to sneak a doughnut, Patches wouldn't budge until she got her share..."*

been waiting for arrived. I'll never forget how nervous I was, wondering whether she'd buck me off. But Patches just looked at me as if to say, "It's about time. Let's go."

I loved riding her early in the morning, just as the sun was coming up. We'd quietly walk down the trails and be greeted by rabbits, lizards, quail and coyotes. I cherished those times.

Patches got to the point where she would feel me shift in the saddle and she would stop. She knew we had arrived at a beautiful plateau, and I wanted to enjoy the view. I think she enjoyed it, too, as we lifted our heads and enjoyed the breeze and the sun on our faces.

There were times I'd drink a cup of coffee during those morning rides. If I tried to sneak a doughnut, she wouldn't budge until she got her share.

When Patches was about 5 years old, I started to ride her in local parades. It was so much fun. Somehow we always seemed to end up right behind a radio station van, and as they blasted their music, Patches would start to dance to

the rhythm and even whinny like she was singing along.

She enjoyed rodeos, too. Once we were selected as Rodeo Princess and Rodeo Queen. The sounds of the carnivals, dances and children never bothered her. She could actually fall asleep right where she stood.

Gentle with Children

Patches' colors attracted children—they liked to touch her and whisper secrets in her ears. Once, a friend's 3-year-old was bound and determined to lead Patches around, and the next thing I knew, the two of them were headed down the road together. Patches was so incredibly gentle with him that she even lowered her head practically to the ground so she could be at the youngster's level.

I remember our last parade together. There were antique cars and tractors, fire trucks, mules and horses—and marching bands trying to sidestep the horse droppings. During the parade, a fire broke out at the other end of town, and the entire parade had to pull to the side of the road to let the fire trucks through. It was quite a sight.

A couple of days later, Patches got colic, and in spite of emergency surgery, we had to put her down. My last memory is of her standing in her stall, looking at me with loving eyes as if to say, "I understand, and it's okay."

God promises Heaven will be a place of eternal joy. A pastor once told me that if you need your pets with you to have that joy, why not. I pray that the pastor is right. ∩

It Was Love at First Sight

By Roy Sheumaker Jr., Columbus, Ohio

Editor's Note: *Roy Sheumaker Sr. wrote this story before he died in 1962. It was edited by his son for future generations of the family to enjoy.*

I spotted a horse named "Win" at an auction. I knew she was the horse for me the moment she entered the ring.

Her alert eyes, clean-lined head and small Thoroughbred ears caught my attention immediately. She also had a slim neck and legs, a heritage she got from her sire, a Standardbred trotter by the name of "Iowa King". Her coat was blood-bay.

Luckily, I was the only bidder interested in a yearling that day, so after a nod of agreement from my partner-brother, Charlie, I made a bid on her, and she was mine. We led her home and turned her out in the pasture with our other unbroken horses.

That day, the broken rope on her halter had no real significance to us. Later, we discovered we didn't have a halter strong enough to tie her.

Win didn't get much attention for the next 2 years. Charlie and I were busy farming and breaking other horses. Then one morning, disaster struck. When I went down to the pasture, Win stood there on three legs—the other had been cut by wire and was a bloody mess. Despite the best care we could give, the foot never did heal right.

Fancied Another Redhead

About this time, my interest turned to another redhead, who influenced my life even more than Win. Her name was Goldie Belle, and she became my wife.

Goldie and Win always maintained some sort of a truce. They seemed to have a mutual respect, but no real liking for one another.

On several occasions, however, they worked together very well. Once, after we homesteaded in northern Montana, our 3-year-old son wandered off from the house and became lost in a wheat field. Goldie and Win found him knocking on the door of a schoolhouse about a quarter mile from home.

Another time, a neighbor's cows got into our wheat, and

Goldie and Win collaborated in chasing them all the way home. Afterward, Win decided to take a drink from a large puddle. She stopped suddenly at the edge of the water and put her head down to drink. Goldie was unceremoniously dumped head over skirts into the puddle.

The prairies of Montana were where Win really came into her own. Though I had broken her to ride before we moved from Iowa, she and I learned to drive and rope cattle together after we moved out West. She was so good at it that a

---

"Goldie was dumped head over skirts into the puddle when Win lowered her head to drink..."

---

cowboy offered me twice what she was worth, bum foot and all. But Win was not for sale at any price.

Win worked well in harness, too, but she never seemed to like it. I searched for a buggy mate for her and eventually matched her up with a sorrel. With the two of them pulling a shiny buggy in a spick-and-span harness, I had the equivalent of a present-day convertible with white sidewalls!

Chased a Coyote

Once, Win and I had the chance to test the endurance of a coyote. We'd been out early in the morning checking cattle, when a coyote jumped up from the tall grass ahead of us. We gave chase, and Win seemed to enjoy it, so I decided to let her run.

Just as we caught up, the coyote dodged under a two-strand barbed wire fence. I slid off, stepped on the bottom wire and pushed the top one up with my shoulder. Win quickly stepped through the opening, and we were on the coyote's tail again. About six fences and 9 miles later, we finally caught him.

We lived 20 miles from town, which meant a 7- to 10-hour trip with a team of horses and a wagonload of wheat, or a 2-hour trip with a light team on a buggy. One evening a neighbor rapped on our door—his wife was very ill and he wanted to borrow our buggy to take her to the doctor. He used Win and our sorrel to pull the buggy, and he later told me they got to town in an hour and 15 minutes!

When we moved back to Iowa, we took Win and nine other horses with us. The last 10 years of Win's life were pretty soft. There were no more long trails and Montana blizzards—just a barn with an open door so she could come and go as she pleased. Her only duty was taking our children to school occasionally.

One morning she was not in the barn. I found her out in the pasture, where, at age 27, she had lain down and gone to sleep one last time.   ∩

Turbulent Times Turned Into Golden Memories

By Cathey Aultman, Seminary, Mississippi

While my father was away fighting for our country in World War II, my mother and I waited for him at Grandfather Hosey's farm.

Granddaddy never owned a vehicle. Instead, he had a favorite saddle horse named "Andy" that was his source of transportation to and from the country store. I still remember him, with his flour sack tied to the saddle horn, riding off down the lane and returning with it filled with supplies. There was always a treat for me nestled somewhere inside.

I got to ride along when Granddaddy rode Andy to the pasture several miles away to salt the cows. My mother often told how my he'd take a pillow along so I could sleep more comfortably on the ride home.

Andy was such a gentle creature, and even after a strenuous day of working cattle, he provided joy by taking me for rides around the farm. There was no need to tether him when I stopped and got off because he'd nibble grass and wait patiently until I was ready to move on. In my mind, I was a glamorous cowgirl like Dale Evans doing trick riding—even though we were slowly meandering through the pasture.

The war years were turbulent times. But for a little girl riding a horse on her grandfather's farm, they were golden days that remain etched in my mind a half century later.   ∩

He Knew What He Was Talking About

By Joyce Lindley, Paoli, Indiana

My parents bought me a yearling horse in 1957, when I was 10. In addition to riding, I enjoyed teaching him tricks…and he was very good at learning them. My favorite was signaling him to shake his head "yes" or "no".

All it took was a slight hand signal from me—with a right hand for yes and a left hand for no. He got so clever at it that when people asked him questions, it appeared he really knew what he was talking about! ∩

JOYCE LINDLEY enjoyed showing off her clever horse's saddlebag full of tricks.

19

When the Car, Truck and Tractor Won't Start, It's Time to Get the Horse

By Vicky Fisher, Olathe, Kansas

I was raised on a dairy farm in northern Illinois and have many wonderful memories of those years. But one winter day when I was 8 really stands out.

Our lane was a half mile long, and most school days, I walked to meet the bus. Or I rode my bike, leaving it in the tall grass until I returned. But when it was raining or snowing, my mother or father would drive me.

On this particular morning, it was windy and bitter cold. Dad went out to the garage to start the car to drive me to the bus, but it wouldn't start. He tried the truck—no luck. Then he went to the machine shed to start the tractor; it wouldn't start either.

I had perfect attendance and didn't want to miss school. So Dad suggested that I ride "Billy" to the end of the lane.

Billy was a black Welsh pony that Dad had bought for me at a farm auction as a surprise when I was 5 years old. (We brought him home in the back of that pickup truck that

> *"I had perfect attendance and didn't want to miss school, so Dad suggested I ride Billy…"*

wouldn't start.) I rode Billy all over the farm—to take lunch to my father and brothers in the field and out to the pasture to bring in the cows for milking. I even rode him around the neighborhood to see my friends. We were a team.

I thought it was a good idea to ride Billy to the bus, but I was concerned how he'd get back to the warmth of his barn stall once I left. Dad assured me that as cold as it was, and as smart as Billy was, he would come back all by himself.

Dad went to the barn to bridle Billy while Mother loaded me down with extra pants, mittens, socks, hat and muffler to keep me warm while I waited for the bus. With all of those clothes on, I shuffled out of the house as best as I could. Any other day I could have swung myself up on Billy's back, but Dad had to hoist my bulky body up that morning.

Then off Billy and I went up the lane. We were walking against the wind, and although my face was covered with the muffler, blowing snow stung my eyes. I had to watch for deep drifts so Billy wouldn't trip. If I fell off, I knew I couldn't get myself back up again.

Finally we reached the end of the lane. I waited and waited for the bus until I was almost ready to ride Billy back to the house to get warm again. But Billy was a gentleman and stood there patiently with me. I stayed on his back to warm my legs.

I filled my time talking to him—reminding him to go straight back to the barn after I left. I told him Dad had promised to leave the barn door open, so he could let himself in where it was warm.

The bus finally came. With a hug and a pat, I shouted "Go home, Billy." As I climbed on the bus, I saw Billy heading in the right direction. But I worried about him all day.

After school, Mom met me at the end of the lane in the car, which Dad had finally gotten started. I was relieved when she told me that Billy had come straight home. I quickly changed my clothes and went to his stall to thank him. I hugged him over and over.

He deserved it. Good old-fashioned horsepower pulled through for me on the day the car, the truck and the tractor wouldn't start. ∩

Ole Red Was Full of Tricks

By Peggy Young, Irvine, Kentucky

O le Red was pretty much like any other pony, stubborn when he wanted to be and cooperative the rest of the time. What made him special besides his solid red color was that he was a Christmas gift to my husband, James, and his brother, Ricky, from their father when they were young.

Ole Red was full of tricks. If he could find a crack in the

"OLE RED would ride in a pickup without a stock rack," says Peggy Young. Below: Her husband, James, helps son Matthew ride the lovable pony.

fence, he could get out of any corral or pasture. James spent many mornings hunting for him, but he never complained. It suited James just fine to be a little late for school!

I remember trying to ride Ole Red to the mailbox one day soon after we were married. He was in one of his stubborn moods and would not go, and I was afraid to nudge him in the sides with my heels because James had taught him to buck when someone pressured him. I didn't want to end up on the ground, so I walked him all the way home.

James also taught Ole Red to lie down, play dead and then rear up. He was easy to haul because he would ride in a pick-

up without a stock rack. James always said that if they were out riding and got tired, he could simply flag down the first person he knew driving a pickup, and Ole Red would hop in the back. Not many ponies would do that.

Our 6-year-old son, Matthew, was able to ride Ole Red and play with him. But our newborn son, Leonard, will not have that pleasure. Ole Red died last winter at 33 years of age.

When Leonard grows up, he'll get to hear the stories and see the pictures and videos of Ole Red and know that he was once a very special part of our family. ∩

22

Dreams Really Can Come True

By Leatha Lockhart, Lewiston, Idaho

My family lived in the city in Southern California in the early 1960s. It was no place for a horse, but I was head over hooves in love with them. From as early as I can remember, I was running around and whinnying like a horse, reading about horses and dreaming that one day I'd have one of my very own.

I made a pest of myself riding my bike to all the stables in the area. I'd beg to clean the stalls, brush the horses or do any other chore that would allow me to be around them. I loved the aromas and the sounds of the stables, and best of all, I loved talking to the horses.

Met a New Friend

The stable closest to our house was half a mile away. I spent hours there each Saturday, just hanging around the horses.

One Saturday, I saw a big beautiful buckskin that had arrived a couple days earlier. I could tell she was gentle by the way she nuzzled the palm of my hand when I offered her treats of grass and grain. It was difficult to leave my new friend that day.

On Sunday, my dad loaded all of us in the car for a drive. I was excited because these drives usually took us into the country, where I could look for horses in the pastures and dream away.

This day was different, however. Dad drove only as far as the stable near our house and pulled in. He said he wanted me to show him the horses, since that was all I ever talked about.

As I was showing him around the stable, he stopped in front of the stall of my new buckskin friend. Next thing I knew, Dad had opened the gate and walked into the stall.

Begged Him to Stop

I was mortified because he was not supposed to be inside the stalls. I knew we'd get into terrible trouble, and I would never be allowed to come back.

It got worse. There was a bridle hanging on the stall post

23

and a saddle on the fence. Dad began saddling the horse.

I was so upset and begged my mother to make Dad stop. But he tacked up the buckskin and walked her out of the stall. As he mounted and rode her down the dirt driveway, I ran to the car crying hysterically. I felt my life was ruined because I'd never be allowed to return to this stable and see my beloved friends.

That's when Dad rode up to me with a huge smile on his face and tears in his eyes. "How do you like your new horse, Leatha?" he asked.

He reached out and clasped my little hand in his big one, pulling me up and seating me behind him in the saddle. As we rode down the dirt driveway on this beautiful horse, I was still sobbing—but now in total elation.

I still cry, 39 years later, when I recall that moment. "Buck" and I went on to make many memories. But that first one was extra special for a 7-year-old girl, who'd just had her dream come true.　　　　　　　　　　　　　　　　　　　　　　　Ω

Horses Had Minds of Their Own

By Nancy Snow, Lebanon, Missouri

My first horse was a gelding, 15 or 16 hands high—much taller than my 12-year-old stature. I'd go to the field with a piece of binder twine, make a halter out of it and lead him to a tree stump. Then I could jump on and ride him to the barn to be bridled and saddled.

This big old horse enjoyed kids. One time when my cousins were visiting, a half dozen of us climbed on and rode up to the house. He was covered with kids from the top of his neck to the end of his rump.

Too bad he wasn't as friendly to adults. One day he cornered Dad in the field—and soon afterward, he was sold.

My second horse was a stud colt named "Star" from our old work mare. He was kept in a fenced-in yard where our garage was located. Star loved to chase Mom from the garage to the yard gate every chance he could get!

The last straw came, however, when Mom looked out the kitchen window and saw him reared up on the trunk of her shiny black Chevy, pawing at his reflection. A few days later, he left the farm to join the rodeo circuit.

After I got married, I made sure my daughters learned to ride and appreciate horses, too. Their ponies had minds of their own—just like my horses did.

For instance, my youngest daughter, Kim, had a pony named "Patches". When Patches got tired of riding, he'd run under the apple tree by the loafing shed on Dad's farm and brush Kim off. Dad finally had to cut down the tree.

All of the horses are gone now. But the fun, laughs and wonderful memories we have of them live on.

Dandy Wasn't a Sweetheart to Everyone

By Heide Zurlinden, Tucson, Arizona

Dandy was a Pinto—just 3 years old when we bought her. There were three little boys playing "army" out in the pasture with Dandy when my husband first saw her. Whenever a boy would run a toy jeep or tank into her hoof, she would gently lift her leg so he could run the vehicle through. Dandy would watch until the boy was safely out of the area before she carefully put her hoof back down. Seeing how gentle she was, my husband bought her on the spot.

Dandy touched many, many lives during her 26 years with us. She loved children. If you put a child on her back, she would walk very carefully—even shift her weight if she felt the child slipping.

However, she wasn't a sweetheart to everyone. If there was an adult who thought he could show her who was boss, Dandy knew it the second he hit the saddle. She never bucked, but she had an interesting way to remind the rider who was really in control. Dandy would feign a rubbery neck and walk cross-legged, like she was drunk. It made the rider look like he didn't know what he was doing.

Once, a friend wanted to ride Dandy because she had such a comfortable "rocking chair" lope. Dandy didn't approve of her rider. So after they'd been loping along at a nice pace, she stopped on a dime—with a nickel's change—and dropped her head to munch on a tiny piece of grass. The rider slid down her neck and onto the ground. Dandy looked down at him as if to say, "Hmmm! How'd that happen?"

DANDY WAS GENTLE around young cowpokes. But she could be down-right ornery with an adult in the saddle.

Raw Eggs Perked Her Right Up

By Elizabeth Hoover Biser, Pittsburgh, Pennsylvania

I was born on a farm near Wolfsville, Maryland 91 years ago. My sister helped my mother with the housework. But Dad called me his tomboy. I milked cows, tended to the horses and helped with all the chores around the farm.

I loved all our horses, but "Pet" was my favorite. I rode her all over the farm to round up the cows to bring them in for milking. We had a chicken that always stayed in the barn, and I fed Pet raw eggs I'd sneak from the nest. She loved them, and they seemed to make her peppy when I rode her. (Sh! I don't think my dad ever found out about this.)

One hot summer day, Dad had been working Pet in a field but quit early to give both himself and the horse a well-deserved rest. In the meantime, my friend rode up and asked me to go for a ride. I saddled Pet, and soon we were riding down a country road.

Made It to the Top

Then my friend suggested we should ride into the mountains to Black Rock. That was fine with me.

The mountains were about 7 miles away, and the trail leading up Black Rock was overgrown and rough. But we made it to the top. What a view! On a clear day, you could see three states from this spot. We sat there admiring the countryside, while our horses grazed in the nice grass.

Suddenly we saw two men coming up the path. We were just young teenagers, and this frightened us. So we hopped on our horses and rode down the mountain as fast as we could.

Pet was wet and sweaty when we got to the bottom of the mountain, and as I neared home, I could see Dad standing by the barn waiting for me. He was not happy. "Where have you been?" he asked. "I wanted to rest that horse today."

I didn't tell Dad we had gone all the way to Black Rock. He would have punished me for sure.

However, I did feel bad that I had taken Pet on such a hard ride after she'd put in a full morning's work in the field. But she perked right up when I treated her to some raw eggs! ○

Nothing Stopped This Pony From Delivering the Mail

By Mae Stuffle, Loogootee, Indiana

Our family of 10 children lived on a 244-acre farm in southern Indiana, where Dad grew wheat, corn and soybeans. He supplemented the crops with hogs, sheep and milk cows.

Mom grew a large garden and raised chickens, so she had "egg money" to buy groceries she couldn't grow. We kids had no idea what a luxury it was to have a pony to ride until years later, when we had horses and ponies for our own children.

Dad bought "Topsy", a big Shetland, for the oldest two boys to use for bringing the cows in from the pasture. She also came in handy for getting the mail, since our mailbox was a mile from the house. She was so smart that as soon as she heard the mail rustle in our hands, she'd lay back her ears and head for the barn.

MAE STUFFLE sits high in the saddle, while friends Helen and Joyce Hugunin stand in front of Topsy in this 1940 photograph.

The best times were when we rode her just for fun—sometimes several of us at a time. We never had a saddle, but that didn't stop us from dreaming we were riding with movie- screen cowboys! ∩

A YOUNG Lisa Boltjes rides Slow Poke (above), while an older Lisa rides her mare, Cody (right).

Ahchoo! Horses Made Her Sneeze

By Lisa Boltjes, Adrian, Minnesota

When I was about 4 years old, my parents bought me "Slow Poke", the sweetest horse anyone could ever own.

Slow Poke was a brown and white Shetland pony and so gentle that any kid could ride him. There was something special about this wonderful little pony, and I loved him so much.

About a year later, I developed asthma and became extremely allergic to horses. It was so bad that we had to sell Slow Poke and our other horses. I was heartbroken to think I'd never see him again.

I never stopped wanting another horse, and time and again, I asked my parents for one. But the answer was always no. When I was 12, after taking allergy shots for years, I could feel myself improving. Still, my parents said no to the idea of another horse.

Two weeks before my 14th birthday, the bus dropped my

29

sister and me off after school as usual. Only on this day when we got to the house, my mother was excitedly waiting for us. She said a two-headed calf had been born while we were at school, and she wanted us to go see it right away.

Birthday Surprise

I was excited and asked all kinds of questions as we hurried to the barn. I ran in, expecting to see my sheep and the cow with her two-headed calf. Well, my sheep were there, but instead of a cow and calf, there stood a horse—my early birthday present. I screamed and ran around the barn in delight. I couldn't believe it!

My new horse was a mare named "Cody". She was 20 years old and extremely shy around other horses—so shy that other horses would push her away from the feed and she wouldn't get enough to eat. For that reason and since her owners didn't ride her anymore, they gave her to us for free. So once again, I had a quiet gentle horse, and she hadn't cost a thing!

Later, I bought another horse so my dad could ride with me and we could join a saddle club together. This gelding, named "Roany", is a big beautiful red roan.

I've had Cody and Roany for almost a year now—and knock on wood, my asthma and allergies haven't bothered me once. ∩

He Traded a Calf for Dixie

By Robert Williams, Plymouth, Wisconsin

One summer when I was growing up on a farm in southwestern Colorado, some cattlemen were driving their herd up to summer range on the Grand Mesa. They left a cow in our pasture because she was too ill to travel. That was a fairly common practice back in the 1930s.

The cow got down and couldn't get back up, so I took food and water to her every morning and evening. One morning I discovered her dead with a newborn live calf at her side. That night, we called the owner to tell him what had happened, and he said I could have the calf for taking care of the cow.

I raised the calf, and in the fall, I traded it to my Uncle Floyd for a little filly named "Dixie". I was about 10 years old, and this was the first horse that was really mine.

I babied Dixie—fed her milk when I fed the calves and curried and played with her all the time. Once, when my grandparents were visiting, they wanted to see her. So I led Dixie up the porch steps and right into the house, much to my mother's consternation.

When it was time to break Dixie to ride, all I had to do was get her used to the saddle and to obey the reins. She never

---

"*I* led Dixie up the porch steps and right into the
house—much to Mother's consternation..."

---

did buck when I rode her—although she did buck off my brother and sister!

Eventually I could gallop her into the pasture to drive the cows in for milking without a bridle. And she'd come to me from as far away as she could hear my whistle.

We could trust her to behave very calmly with my two little nieces on her back. But as soon as I climbed on her, she would really show her spirit.

Dixie was a beautiful animal and grew to about 14 hands tall. She was coal black, except for a tiny white spot in the center of her forehead. I was always proud of the way people looked at her when I rode through town.

Sometimes after seeing a Western movie, I'd try the stunts the actors performed—like bouncing my feet on the ground and then swinging over the saddle to touch the ground on the other side while the horse was running. Our horses were trained to stop when we got off, so I suffered quite a few bumps and bruises before Dixie got the idea that this was a different game.

I often think Dixie taught me more than I taught her. It was a great experience growing up with an animal like her. I wish my boys had such an opportunity. ○

Scout's Last Social Appearance

By J. Chesser, Camino, California

I bought "Scout" at a horse auction in 1967. He was a beautiful sorrel with a golden red tail and mane that caught my eye as he was prancing about.

Scout traveled home fairly well in the trailer that day, but I had quite a surprise the next day, when he kicked and bit and wouldn't allow me to get close. I figure he must have been abused.

With the help of friends, I was eventually able to work the meanness out of him. But Scout remained a spirited challenge over the years, and I had many thrilling rides.

Once, I was riding bareback when the reins became tangled in his mane. He ran full out in the direction of the barn, jumping a stream along the way. It was all I could do to hang on—let alone untangle the reins to stop him. Luckily, a bright colored car caught his eye as we approached the highway, and he stopped.

Almost Took a Tumble

Another time, he reared up with me on his back. Then, while on his hind feet, he somehow jumped forward. My blue jeans were damp with his sweat and kept me from sliding. Otherwise, I'd have taken a tumble.

I still call Scout the fastest horse in the West. My daughter Shawn used to ride him in races with her friends, and Scout would always win. He loved to run and couldn't stand to be passed up.

One time we entered Scout in a barrel race, and Shawn tried to take him

SCOUT COULD BE a handful with a person onboard, but he sure didn't mind giving this cute little pup a ride.

through the course. Scout had his own ideas and ran the course backward, then went to the center of the ring and proudly reared up. This was his last social appearance!

Scout is 35 and retired. But he still looks good and continues to eat…er, like a horse.   ∩

TRACY SYOEN knew as soon as she met this Quarter Horse named Shad that they would be best friends.

Sixth Sense Turned Into Horse Sense

By Tracy Syoen, Woodridge, Illinois

At age 15 and without a lot of cash, I went searching for the horse of my dreams. I wanted a well-started horse that I could teach complicated riding skills. Sometimes I think I have a sixth sense about things, and the moment I saw a Quarter Horse named "Shad", I just knew he was the horse for me.

My parents didn't live on a farm, so I had to board Shad. It took all my baby-sitting money to pay for his upkeep, but I didn't mind.

After all, I had just what I wanted—a chance to train a horse and a chance to learn from him, all at the same time. Shad was just what I needed, too, to help me handle the transition into high school. As corny as it may sound, Shad truly was my best friend during that difficult time in my life.

The morning of my first horse show, my mom and I were giving Shad a bath when I noticed a small scab on one of his back legs. But it was small, and I thought nothing more about it at the time.

I didn't know what to expect when I entered the show ring. I soon discovered that, in spite of all the time I had spent training, Shad was greener than I'd bargained for. I considered myself lucky when I got him to do a decent barrel pattern that day without bucking.

However, I didn't mind. I knew I had more learning and training to do than I had ever imagined, and I was ready for the challenge.

Shad Was Lame

When I arrived home from school the Friday following the horse show, my mom was just hanging up the phone. I immediately knew there was a problem—my sixth sense again. "What's wrong with Shad?" I cried.

The veterinarian had been out to the stable to check on another horse, and while he was there, Shad limped up to the barn dead lame. The vet did some tests and suspected Shad had an infected joint, especially after finding the tiny scab on his leg.

I went to see Shad and found him standing in his stall. His nose was touching the ground and his back leg was lifted so it was barely touching. He was covered with sweat and so miserable that I don't think he even knew I was there.

The next day, we nervously called the horse clinic for the results of the tests. The vet was right—Shad had an infected joint. Luckily, it was discovered early enough that it could possibly be treated with surgery. But there was no guarantee. Even if the surgery worked, they told me Shad might never be fully sound again.

Surgery Was Risky

My parents said they would pay for the surgery—if I wanted to proceed. Or we could put him down and begin looking for another horse. It was my decision.

Well, I didn't want another horse. I wanted Shad. I wasn't finished training him, and he wasn't done teaching me either. So we took him to the clinic for surgery.

I was so scared. That night, I prayed harder than I have ever prayed before. I spent 2 hours on my knees and another 2 in my bed telling God how important Shad was to me.

Dad woke me up the next day to tell me the vet had just called. Shad had responded so well to antibiotics overnight that they decided not to perform the surgery! They kept him on antibiotics at the clinic for a week and then sent him home. Tears of joy streamed down my face when I led him to the trailer that day.

A Silver Lining

Shad was stall-bound for a month and then spent even more time recuperating in the pasture. Finally one day, the vet said, "I think it's about time you saddled your horse."

I was so thankful, because Shad had fully recovered when the odds were against him. It was nothing short of a miracle.

They say there's a silver lining in every cloud, and I believe it. You see, during the months while Shad was in recovery, I spent every day changing his bandages and grooming him.

We formed a bond and learned to really trust one another—something we lacked when we entered that first horse show.

Now we're a team... running barrels and jumping fences with confidence. More importantly, Shad has patiently taught me so much about training horses. I'm even planning to pursue it as a career. ∩

LOVINGLY GROOMING Shad helped Tracy Syoen nurture a special bond with him.

She Met Her Dream Horse by Accident

By Karen Marvin, Fredericktown, Ohio

My husband, Randy, and I bought a failing grocery store in Johnsonville, Ohio a few years ago. We worked long nights there trying to get the store back on its feet. During the day we had other jobs to pay the bills, and my sister Pam ran the store for us.

One April night, 4 months after we bought the store, I heard a terrible crash while I was closing up. I ran to the door and saw a horse laying flat on the road in front of the store. Nearby an Amish buggy was flipped on its side, and people were climbing from the car that was also involved in the accident.

I yelled at Randy to help as I ran to the phone to call 911. I explained to the operator that we needed a veterinarian as well as an ambulance.

By the time I got to the scene, Jonas, the owner of the buggy, was unhitching the horse's harness. The horse heaved herself up and stood in the road looking dazed. I offered to hold her while Jonas answered questions for the patrolman who'd come to investigate. Jonas seemed grateful and told me the horse's name was "Frosty".

I led Frosty to our yard and walked her back and forth. I picked glass out of her leg and shoulder and brushed the pea gravel off her side. All the time I was talking with her, pleading with her not to go into shock.

Leg Wasn't Broken

Frosty limped a little, but her leg did not appear to be broken. She had the sweetest personality and was so gentle. I couldn't help but bond with her.

A couple hours later, someone brought a truck and trailer to haul Frosty home. It was then that I learned the details of the accident and realized Frosty was a very lucky horse.

Jonas normally makes a left turn at the road in front of our store. But that night, he wasn't planning on going home right away and intended to continue straight down the road. Frosty must have been ready for her oats and turned left anyway—right into the path of the oncoming car. She hit the hood, bounced over the roof, slid down the trunk and onto the road. I'll never forget the sound of the crash.

Over the next few weeks, Jonas became one of the customers at our store. When he came, I'd hurry outside to pet

> "*Frosty was ready for her oats and turned right into the path of an oncoming car...*"

Frosty and see how her cuts were healing. I had grown up on a farm and always loved animals, and I even dreamed of owning a horse someday. So I told Jonas that if he ever wanted to sell Frosty, to please let me be the first to know.

Jonas came into the store one October evening, about a year and half later, and asked me if I still wanted to buy Frosty. I said, "Oh, yes!" and then picked up a penny on the floor. I handed it to him and laughingly asked, "Can I use this for a down payment?"

Randy had quit his job to work full-time at the store, and I was still working my day job to pay the bills. So after a couple weeks of trying to justify buying Frosty, I finally told Randy to tell Jonas the next time he came into the store that we simply couldn't afford to buy her. It broke my heart.

Merry Christmas!

I was at home the Saturday morning before Christmas, when our dogs started barking like crazy. I went to the back door to see what was causing the commotion. There, coming around the back of the house were my two sisters and brothers-in-law with silly grins on their faces.

They were leading a horse. "You know who this is, don't you?" they said. "It's Frosty!"

Randy was minding the store, so he had them deliver my Christmas gift for him. It was my best present ever.

I learned a lot about Frosty that winter. I discovered that she didn't like windy days, and I could tell by her reactions if a storm was brewing. Jonas had warned me that she loved to roll on the ground…and one day when I was leading her through some fresh snow, she dropped to the ground and started making her version of a snow angel.

Frosty was a racehorse in her younger days and enjoyed trotting up and down the lane. Once summer arrived, I turned her out in the pasture with the cows, where she could really kick up her heels.

After a stressful day in the store, it's such a joy to go out to the pasture and watch her enjoy her retirement. ∩

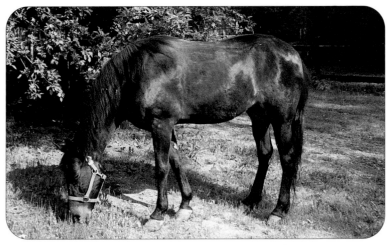

FROSTY is enjoying the slower pace of retirement out in the pasture.

Dolly Meets a Doll of a Horse

By Dolly Stubbert, Dayton, Washington

A few years ago, I moved to a small town in western Washington. To my surprise and delight, I found four horses pastured in the small lot next to my new apartment.

I proceeded to make friends with all of them, but my favorite was a small Appaloosa mare. She was reddish in color with white spots on her rump and a large star on her forehead. So I called her "Star". She'd come to me every time I called her by that name.

Weeks went by before I met her owner. I told her what I'd been calling the horse. She laughed and said, "Oh, no. Her name is 'Dolly'."

I got quite a kick out of that. You see, that's my name!   ∩

A Double Dose of Blessings

By Cyndy Nelson, Hancock, Maryland

D uring the 10 years I've worked at Apple Valley Ranch, I've ridden many horses, and even broke a few. But my special blessing was making friends with two Appaloosa geldings.

I met "Apple Jack" when I first started working at the ranch. He was stunning, mostly white with a shading of black on his face, neck and four legs. He had black spots on his rump and a white blaze on his forehead. He was the kind of horse you were proud to be seen riding.

I knew I liked Jack the first time I rode him. He was spirited, but not a spooky horse. New places and things didn't bother him. Sometimes I could tell he wanted to go his own way, but he always listened to me instead. We became a team, and I felt at ease riding him alone over all the ranch's wooded trails.

Any time life became stressful for me, there was nothing so refreshing as a good ride on Jack. When you're on a good horse in the woods, alone with God and enjoying His creation, the hustle and bustle of life comes to a screeching halt. It's a soothing tonic.

When Jack had to be put down one dreary January day because of a foot injury, I hugged him one last time—convinced I would never have another special horse friend like him. I was wrong!

Wasn't Much to Look at

That spring, the ranch owner and I drove over an hour to look at an Appaloosa named "Pepper". He wasn't a particularly good-looking horse the first time I laid eyes on him. In fact, he was so scrawny we thought we had wasted the trip.

But we decided to ride him anyway. Pepper's wonderful disposition and gentle spirit won us over immediately, and we took him home to the ranch.

Pepper put on a good deal of weight and eventually blossomed. He's also become a great trail horse. He and I go exploring and have discovered some sights Jack and I had missed. We have ridden through the woods and up into the mountains and have seen deer, groves of dogwoods, wild turkeys in flight and incredible panoramic views.

Pepper isn't a fireball like Jack. He's very easygoing and gentle, and he has a calming effect on spooky horses that may be on the trail with us.

Sometimes Pepper nudges me because he wants his head rubbed. That reminds me of Jack—he loved to have his head rubbed, too.

I feel blessed to have had two special horse friends in my life. ♘

APPLE JACK strikes a cool pose in the snow (top), while Cyndy Nelson puts Pepper through his paces (left).

40

Ginger Spiced Up Their Christmas

By Delores Jilson Morgan, Elmira, New York

Back in 1945, my family lived on a beautiful farm. Our farmhouse was an old stagecoach stopover. It had many rooms, but only three were heated. The kitchen had two cookstoves in it, and the living room had a woodstove.

On Christmas morning that year, the eight of us were opening our gifts. I got a cowboy hat and boots, which I donned and modeled in my pj's. Then my father asked me to go into the kitchen to get something for him.

Wow!!! Standing there eating hay and oats from the kitchen table was a beautiful Shetland pony named "Ginger". I rode her into the living room, and we all had a good laugh.

When I was 11, I was given another horse, named "Spot". He had been abused, and I wasn't able to ride him for a year. But eventually I could ride him on my paper route and to get the cows.

These animals are just two of many joys the Lord has provided me over the years.   ∩

Pansy Was a Pretty Sight

By Sidney Coombs, Garden City, Kansas

I was raised on a North Dakota farm with three older sisters. When I was 4 years old, Dad thought we ought to get a pony. He made a deal with the John Deere dealer in McClusky and brought home a red roan pony we named "Pansy".

We kids loved riding Pansy and got along fine with her. However, she had one characteristic that did not set well with Dad—she was impossible to catch in an open field. Dad got to the point where he could not stand chasing Pansy anymore. So without telling us kids, he sold her to a neighbor.

After a few days of listening to four howling kids, Dad decided it was easier to put up with Pansy. So he went and brought her home. What a pretty sight she was!   ∩

She Rode Smoky Up to Seventh Heaven

By Lucille Wohler, Clay Center, Kansas

As a child, I desperately wanted a pony. This was the 1930s, though, and there was no way my parents could afford to buy me one. We had draft horses for fieldwork, so the only riding I did was taking them the short distance from the water tank to the barn.

When my parents moved to a different farm with a larger pasture, they finally decided we needed a riding horse to bring the cows in to milk. About that time, a relative was moving to town and did not want to sell his Shetland pony, "Smoky". He said we could "borrow" him if we fed and sheltered him. I was in seventh heaven.

For 5 years, Smoky and I had fun. It was exhilarating to split the breeze as he ran through the meadows and pastures. I only hope he enjoyed it as much as I did.

Shetland ponies can be a bit on the stubborn side, but not Smoky. He had a great disposition. Several children could pile on him and he'd never rear, buck or kick.

When my father passed away, my mother and I moved to town, and Smoky was returned to his former owner. I never knew where he went after that, but I'm confident he gave some other family as much pleasure as he did me.

I was an only child, and I'll never forget my short time with this wonderful companion.   ∩

The Best Wedding Present

By Carolyn Miller, Green Ridge, Missouri

I was a town girl who'd always dreamed of owning a horse. So when I got married to a farm boy in 1962, he bought me a 9-month-old black and white filly.

She was sweet and gentle, and we called her "Soxie" be-

SOXIE STRUTS before the camera to show off her three white feet for which she was named. She was also the lead horse in the parades at the Missouri State Fair.

cause she had three white feet. As the years went by and I became a more experienced horse person, I began to realize just how special Soxie was. We never had to break her. We just got on her when she was 2 years old and took off down the road.

Much to my mother-in-law's dismay, my husband took our 2-week-old daughter for a ride on Soxie. But they didn't have a lick of a problem.

Soxie and I rode in a lot of parades and on many trail rides. One of our most memorable experiences was the year Soxie served as the lead horse in all of the parades at the Missouri State Fair.

Before the surrey races, our job was to lead each group of horses into the ring. The temperature was extremely hot that day, and Soxie was expected to perform at a gallop. After one race, she was so wet with sweat that the saddle slid under her belly, and I tumbled to the ground—right in front of a grandstand full of people! Soxie just stood there and waited for me to get up and regain my composure and dignity.

Our two children showed Soxie in 4-H. The fun and pleasure she gave all of us cannot be measured.

She also gave us three babies. One was a pure white colt; the other two were bay fillies. I still have one of the bay fillies, and she had a black and white colt that looks like his grandma.

Soxie was 28 when we lost her. But it's a thrill seeing the two generations of her offspring in our field. And when I think of all of the memories and lessons of life she provided me and our children, that 9-month-old Paint filly was the best wedding present ever.   ∩

Fox Was a Tricky One

By Marguerite Thompson, Ottawa, Illinois

My father was a dairy farmer, so my sister and I grew up around dairy cattle, horses and other farm animals. But of all the animals we knew, a small black pony that Dad bought for us will always be special in our memories.

We named our pony "Fox", and that turned out to be a fitting name because she was full of sly tricks. We always had to be on guard for her foxy ways.

One of her favorite tricks was swelling her stomach when we saddled her. Then when we settled into the saddle to ride, she'd let the air out, which, of course, made the saddle too loose. It would slip sideways, and we usually ended up on the ground.

We also had to remember that Fox didn't like to cross the railroad tracks near the farm. She'd run like lightning down the road until she came to the tracks. Then she'd stop on all fours. If we weren't prepared, we'd find ourselves plummeting over her head.

Fox was very small. So when she had a colt, it was especially tiny. I can still recall the many people who stopped on the road along our pasture to admire Fox and her darling little baby.   ∩

Wherever Patch Goes, Phoebe Follows

By Hailey Tomlinson, Delta Junction, Alaska

Our family lives on a 320-acre farm in Alaska, where we keep a number of horses. But "Patch", a Mustang/Paint gelding, and "Phoebe", an Appaloosa mare, are the most special.

These two will simply not be parted. Wherever one goes, the other follows. It's next to impossible to take one out for a ride without also bridling the other. Their loyalty to one another never ceases to amaze me.

PHOEBE and PATCH graze side by side, content when they're together.

I remember the day we went to pick them up a couple of years ago. We snapped a lead rope onto Phoebe's halter to load her into the trailer. She was reluctant to leave her friend Patch. Patch was even more upset. He kicked and bucked all around the corral—quite a display for a 30-year-old horse—before we caught him and loaded him into the trailer, too.

We staked this inseparable pair out in a grassy plot near our garden. After a few days of grooming, treats and TLC, they warmed up to us. So Dad decided to lead Patch out to the pasture with my 4-year-old brother, Nicholas, in the saddle.

Sturdy Stake Didn't Stop Her

Phoebe, still staked out in the garden, began to whinny and pull on her rope with all her might. My sister and I tried to comfort her, but she pulled the sturdy stake right out of the ground. Off she flew for a happy reconciliation with Patch.

Another time, my sister Meghan took Phoebe for a ride—or at least tried to. A little ways down the trail, Phoebe dug her heels into the ground and refused to take another step.

When they got back home, Patch was standing in a deserted corner of the corral with a grief-stricken look on his face. When Phoebe came into view, they both whinnied for joy…and when Phoebe was turned loose in the corral, she trotted over to Patch and the two began nibbling each other's mane and exchanging horse kisses.

Even now as I write this, Patch and Phoebe are cuddled cozily together in the snow-laden corral, under the silvery light of the Alaska moon. They're probably dreaming of all the fun they'll have running in the grassy fields next summer. But whatever they do, they'll undoubtedly do it together.   ∩

Best Friends Stick Together

By Nicole Govero, Festus, Missouri

My love for horses began when I was about 3 years old. But there was a problem. We lived in town, so buying a horse was out of the question (and I knew I could not fit a horse under my bed). But I prayed about it every night and read every horse book I could get my hands on.

The day I turned 14, we moved to a place in the country with 85 acres of pasture and woods. In less than 6 months, I had my very own horse.

She was a 4-year-old Quarter Horse mare named "Katie". But unfortunately, Katie was not the friend I was hoping she'd be. She was very stubborn and hard to handle, and after a year, I

A LITTLE GENTLENESS helped Katie overcome a rocky start.

still couldn't control her enough to take her out riding.

I grew so frustrated that I put Katie up for sale. But when people came to look at her, it made me realize how much I loved her. So I decided not to sell her.

Instead, I went to a trainer, who taught me how to correct her problems using gentle methods. Katie and I learned to work with each other, and now we're best friends.

Money couldn't make me part with Katie today. After all, best friends stick together. ◠

A Rooster Tale

By Jenny Alred, Argyle, Texas

Rooster is a Quarter Horse I raised from a colt. I gave him that name because he's so cocky!

My daughter Mindy and I were riding along the side of the highway one day when she was about 7 years old. She was riding her horse, "Comanche", and I was on Rooster.

Suddenly I saw a dog leap over the railroad tracks and run toward us. It scared Rooster, who took off running so hard it threw me back in the saddle and caused me to pull back hard on the reins. Rooster had no place to go but straight up, and when he reared, I slid to the ground.

Mindy was scared to death that I was hurt and screamed, "Mama! Are you all right?" I had the breath knocked out of me, so I could barely answer.

While I was struggling to my feet, I heard Rooster's hooves pounding the pavement as he ran down the middle of the highway. I could see cars coming at him from both directions.

There was no way I could run and catch him. So I hollered out, "Rooster! Where do you think you're going?"

To my amazement, he stopped dead in his tracks, looked back at me and whinnied. Then he ran right up to me and stopped at my feet.

Mindy and I were shocked. I looked at her and said, "I don't believe it. This only happens in the movies!"

I got back on Rooster and counted my lucky stars. Then we rode uneventfully back home. ◠

Shy Horse Looked to Her for Protection

By Mona Gourley, Butler, Pennsylvania

Ever since I was young, I wanted a horse. But we lived in Seattle and were quite poor. The best I could do was save my baby-sitting money and occasionally go to a riding stable for lessons.

My husband and I had been married for several years and had three children, when we moved to a rural area in western Pennsylvania. Our neighbor boarded horses and told us about one that was for sale. My husband bought him for me—my anniversary, birthday and Christmas presents all wrapped up together in a beautiful dun-colored Appaloosa named "Sundown". It was the best present I ever received.

MONA GOURLEY loves to take her granddaughter Dylan for a ride around the pasture on Sundown.

The kids and I rode Sundown nearly every day. Our backyard almost adjoined the pasture where he lived with six other horses.

Very quickly he learned to come when I called him. Eventually, I didn't even have to call—he met me at the gate when he spotted me walking toward the pasture.

Sundown loved humans, but he was easily spooked by other horses. They bullied him, and even smaller horses chased him. It got worse when a white Arabian named

49

"Zoltan" came to live at the stable. He constantly picked on Sundown, and even though Sundown was bigger and faster, he was terrified of Zoltan.

It even got to the point where Sundown wouldn't come when I called him. He'd hide in the wooded area of the pasture—too afraid to walk past Zoltan to the gate. I had to go out to get him, carrying a stick to keep Zoltan away. Only then would Sundown come out of the woods.

It was a ridiculous-looking spectacle—all 125 pounds of me keeping these 1,000-pound animals apart. But it made me feel good that my baby, Sundown, trusted me to protect him!

Zoltan is gone now, and at 28, Sundown is being eased into retirement. But he's still my baby, and I love him dearly. ∩

Dixie Left the Model T In Her Dust

By Altha Wilkerson, Hico, Texas

I'm almost 85 years old and have loved horses ever since Papa began taking me with him to the barn to feed them. He'd lift me up and put me in a feed trough, where they wouldn't step on my toes. There I'd stand and pet their heads while they ate.

I rode them as soon as I was old enough to sit on their backs while Papa led them to the water. Maybe that explains why I was able to handle "Dixie", the horse I rode 3 miles to school.

Dixie was a stubborn mare, determined to always be in charge. She did not like to leave home in the morning, and she was always eager to get home after school. One afternoon when I was riding home from high school, two boys in a Model T passed us and yelled, "Come on! Let's race."

That was all Dixie needed. Away we flew—leaving the Model T in our dust. We were halfway home before I was able to get her under control.

Just then the Model T passed us. Dixie was off again, and I didn't get her under control until we reached home. I had a wild 3-mile ride that day! ∩

Golden Memories of
A Horse Named Silver

By Shelley Meier, Lone Jack, Missouri

My aunt and uncle lived on a dairy farm in southern Missouri, 200 miles from my home. My brother, sister and I spent our summers and holidays with them, and that's where I learned to ride "Silver", my cousins' patient gelding.

When I was small, I'd grab Silver's mane and put my foot on his knee to climb on. Sometimes this took me a while. But Silver didn't mind.

He did love to run, though. If you got him to gallop, he thought he had a race to win!

Silver was especially good at bringing in the cows for milking. All you had to do was sit on his back and let him do the work. He'd follow the cows and could turn on a dime to get them back in line if they tried to get away.

Occasionally my two cousins, my sister, brother and I all rode Silver at the same time. He took it in stride, but the person riding in back always had a difficult time staying on, especially going uphill! ∩

Julie Habel

51

SADDLED UP and ready to ride Pat through the streets of Wisconsin Rapids, Wisconsin for the annual high school homecoming parade is Roy Knuteson in the '30s.

Dad Traded an Old Axle for Pat

By Roy Knuteson, Fort Collins, Colorado

The first time I saw "Pat", he was staked out at Wolcott's Auto Wrecking Yard in Wisconsin Rapids, Wisconsin. Someone had traded this derelict white horse bearing a Western brand for some used car parts. Back in 1939, this was a common practice, as people would trade for almost anything.

Pat was a thin, pathetic-looking gelding that had obviously been neglected. But he was as gentle as a kitten. My 11-year-old heart went out to this poor animal.

I pleaded with Dad to purchase him so we could properly care for him and I could have my first riding horse. The next day, I came home to find Pat in our pasture. Dad had traded an old car front axle and $15 to get him.

Thanks to lots of alfalfa and clover hay and generous rations of oats, Pat quickly regained his weight, and with it, his appearance and pep. He became my special charge and

52

friend. I bought a World War I-surplus McClellan Army saddle from Montgomery Wards for $4.75 and began to ride Pat almost daily. He also became a fine trotter on our buggy and two-wheeled sulky cart.

Little did we know, however, that Pat had a wild streak, and it began to manifest itself with increasing frequency. I was

---

"All too often, I would have to lead Pat home after he bucked me off..."

---

asked to ride in the annual high school homecoming parade, and Pat nervously pranced his way down the entire downtown parade route. My mother almost fainted when she saw how agitated he was.

Then Pat began running the length of our pasture and jumping over the fence. So I'd have to track him down.

When he was feeling his oats, he wouldn't even let me ride him anymore. All too often, I'd have to lead him home after he bucked me off and wouldn't allow me to remount.

We blamed his erratic behavior on his maverick heritage. Finally, we had no choice but to sell him to a man who assured us he could handle all kinds of horses.

It was sad selling this once-emaciated horse that we nourished back to health. But it was worth the sadness because of all the fond memories I have to this day.   ∩

She Hasn't Been on a Horse Since

By Lorraine La Plante, Eatonville, Washington

I always wanted a horse when I was young, but the closest I ever got to one was watching cowboy movies as a kid at our local movie theater.

Eventually, we bought a horse named "Shorty" for our 10-year-old daughter, Connie. As his name suggested, Shorty was small and scraggly. But he was very gentle and easy to handle—provided you knew how to ride.

One day he was saddled, and I hopped on for my first

horseback ride. I decided to go to my mother's house a few blocks away, and we were doing fine until I said, "Whoa!"

Shorty just kept on going. As I rode by unable to stop, I yelled to my mother that I'd call her later—if I made it home!

I haven't been on a horse since. But I sit in the bleachers and burst with pride as I watch my granddaughter, Cindy Snowden, win awards galore for her horsemanship.

CINDY SNOWDEN (right) is an accomplished horsewoman, says her proud grandma, Lorraine La Plante.

Pony Was Tied To the Christmas Tree

By Faye Clark, Athens, Tennessee

Folks called my grandfather Doctor Joe. He was a physician who owned a small hospital in Loudon, Tennessee and made house calls with his horse and buggy. We lived right across the street, and I made house calls with him as soon as I could sit up.

Doctor Joe loved horses and raised Standardbreds for racing as well as his transportation. On my third Christmas, he surprised me with a black Shetland pony tied to the Christmas tree with a big red ribbon. I named her "Merry Christmas".

Doctor Joe hired the hospital cook's son to feed and groom the pony and to accompany me while I was riding. We went all over downtown Loudon and stopped at the drugstore every day, where he bought three ice cream cones—one for me, one for him and one for Merry Christmas.

Doctor Joe was always master of ceremonies at the local

horse shows. Merry Christmas and I got to be the mascots.

After Doctor Joe's death in 1935, my family moved to Knoxville. Merry Christmas stayed behind at my uncle's farm near Loudon. But when I was 14, I got a job teaching riding lessons at a stable, so we moved Merry Christmas there. Again, she went to all the horse shows with me. I even taught her to jump low fences when she was 18.

When Merry Christmas was 20, I loaned her to a policeman who had a 3-year-old granddaughter. Merry Christmas lived out her days in their backyard barn and once again had a small child to love her as much as I did.

Ironically Merry Christmas died peacefully in her sleep on Christmas Day, when she was 25 years old. ∩

Penny Gave a Dollar's Worth of Effort

By Mary French, Hulett, Wyoming

Penny was half Arabian and half Quarter Horse. Of all the horses I've owned, she was the smartest and the most willing and honest.

She was an excellent stock horse. If we were driving cattle and I had to stop to open the gate, Penny would never take her eyes off them. When I got back on her, she was ready to herd them through the gate and knew exactly what to do.

One time I climbed on Penny bareback to put a cow in the corral. She did not want to work that way and tried to buck me off. After I got her under control, I dismounted and put a saddle on her, like I should have in the first place. Then she happily cooperated with me. ∩

MARY FRENCH and Penny made quite a team.

Modern-Day Schoolgirl Rides Her Pony to Class

By Holly Roberts, Nobleboro, Maine

RUBAN is in a class all by himself.

My first horse, "Ruban", is a sweet plucky pony…and 2 years ago, when I was 11 years old, my grandfather suggested I ride him to school.

He had good friends who owned a farm across the street from the school, and Ruban could spend the school day there. So the very next morning, Ruban and I left for school at 6 a.m. We got there about 7:30.

We did this several times a week. Ruban, who was about 11 years old, loved the attention and exercise.

After a while, I became weary of wearing my backpack full of books while I rode. So my grandfather bought a cart, painted it bright blue and decorated it with orange reflective tape that could be easily seen in traffic. Ruban pulled the cart tirelessly to school each morning and afternoon for the rest of the school year.

Then Grandfather and I noticed Ruban was wheezing. The veterinarian checked him over and discovered he had heaves. Ruban could no longer be used for hard work around the farm, but because I was so small, the vet said I could still ride or drive him to school.

By the end of the summer, however, I experienced a growth spurt. I gained 30 pounds and grew 6 inches in 5 months—too much to ride Ruban in his condition.

Now I have a new horse that I ride to school, a registered Morgan named "Sandy".

I still have Ruban, too. Sometimes people ask me why I don't sell him, since I can't ride him. But I would never sell my first horse. A first horse is like a girl's first love!

He Rode Guard Duty Around the Atomic Bomb

By George Heger, Waterford, Michigan

I was one of 125 military police who had taken calvary training in World War II. We were sent to Los Alamos, New Mexico early in 1943 to ride guard duty around areas where the atomic bomb was being made.

We rode 8 hours at a time on swing shifts, day and night. Our stable of horses was large, and a fresh horse was assigned to us each shift.

My favorite was "Silver", a gray and white rascal who was very proud. He, too, served his country in time of need. ∩

GEORGE HEGER'S favorite mount was a proud patriot named Silver.

Finally—a Horse of Her Own

By Joanne Schudda, Darlington, Wisconsin

M om used to joke that my first word was "horse"! I was a city girl whose heart has always belonged to the country. My first experience on a horse was when I was 4 and visited my Aunt Elsie's farm. The horse's name was "Judy".

I was 12 before I had the opportunity to ride again—other than pony rides at the carnival. My dad had a friend who owned a pony farm just outside of town. I made friends with some of the kids who boarded their ponies there, and for the next two summers, I spent every chance I could riding. We rode through the woods, put together mock horse shows and had just plain fun.

The next few years, I spent all my baby-sitting money at the local riding stable. I was such a regular that they let my friends and me go out without a guide. I always rode a horse named "Barney".

Then I got married and had a daughter. There was little opportunity to do any riding until we rented a place in the country. We met some friends who owned horses, and they invited me on a trail ride. I was back in the saddle again, but it was still on a borrowed horse.

Surprised Her with a Pony

When I was 31, my husband, Doug, surprised me with my first horse of my own, a little black Welsh mix named "Babe". She was a difficult horse to catch, but after I learned her quirks, she was a good ride.

Babe was really better with younger kids. So after I acquired my second horse, "Snake River Midget", I gave Babe to some friends whose children just loved her. (My daughter was afraid of horses!)

Snake was bred when I got her and soon brought "Lacy" into the world. Lacy was my baby. When I'd sit in the yard and watch Snake graze, Lacy would try to sit in my lap. She also followed me around like a puppy. I'm not sure she knew she was a horse.

When it was time to train her, I was able to do it myself, even though I had never trained a horse before. She did every-

IT WAS a proud moment for Joanne Schudda's granddaughter, Karla, when she got to sit atop Lacy. Now Karla has a horse of her own, too, so they can go trail riding together.

thing I asked of her with very little argument or fuss.

We lost Snake in an accident when Lacy was 9 months old. Doug bought me "Texas", a Palomino gelding, so I would not have to give up riding while Lacy was still a baby.

The years have passed and now I have a granddaughter, Karla, who loves horses as much as I do. I didn't want her to wait as long as I did for a horse of her own, so we bought her a little black and white Paint named "Baby Blue".

It's a lot of fun riding with my granddaughter. My daughter has even started riding. As for Doug, he prefers horsepower in the form of his motorcycle! ◠

Thunderbolt's Still Surrounded By Adoring Children

By Andrea Dean Van Scoyoc, New Port Richey, Florida

I'm a country girl transplanted in the city. My years in the city, unfortunately, have been many more than my years in the country. But I will never forget my coal-black pony, "Thunderbolt".

I was only about 3 years old when we got Thunderbolt, so I don't remember the exact circumstances of his coming to live with us, but I was very happy he did. I loved his shaggy mane and squat muscular body. I was thrilled when I could help my father saddle him. I'll never forget the wonderful aroma of that leather saddle.

I was much too small to ride Thunderbolt by myself, and he was a bit cantankerous. So my father would lead him around the yard for me. I felt so grown-up sitting in the saddle and looking out across the pasture next to our house.

It was a sad day when we had to sell Thunderbolt. But he went to a children's home, and my father assured me that the children loved him as much as I did.

That was 25 years ago. My parents sold the pasture not long afterward, and apartments now occupy the land. The quiet road we lived on is now a major thoroughfare.

But if I close my eyes, I can still see my little pony—his shaggy head bent low to the ground contentedly munching grass out in the pasture. Somehow I know he's in horse heaven, in his very own pasture, surrounded by adoring children. ♘

Ol' Ted Outsmarted Himself

By Lowry Ingrum, Porterville, California

We had a horse named "Ted" who loved to escape from the barnyard—until we fooled him into turning around and coming home again.

That was back in the days when my father-in-law kept his Model T in the barn. He had to open the barnyard gate to drive out, and ol' Ted just waited for that moment to escape.

One winter day when the gate was opened to get the car out, Ted, with ears laid back, galloped through the gate to freedom. My father-in-law yelled, "Get back here, Ted!"

At that exact moment, Ted hit the wooden bridge that spanned the ditch. It was icy, and he slipped and fell.

Ted turned and looked at my father-in-law as if to say, "Why did you do that to me?" Then he got up, hung his head and walked back into the barnyard.

For years after that incident, all you had to do was yell to Ted just before he hit the bridge. He'd meekly turn around and walk back to the barnyard. ♘

Lynn M. Stone

Old Photos Bring Back Memories

By Donna Rine Deem, Fort Mill, South Carolina

When I was a freshman in high school, Dad and my Uncle Bob built a barn. After we painted it bright "barn red", we started looking for a horse for me.

I was excited—but a little scared, too, because I'd never been around horses before. We went to the fairgrounds, where we saw "Buffy". She was a spirited 5-year-old Appaloosa and the biggest horse I'd ever seen.

We bought Buffy, and she became my main focus. Before school every morning, I'd roll out of bed and head for the barn, still in my nightgown, to clean, feed and water her before I left for the day.

As soon as school was over, I hurried home to see her. Buffy would be looking over the fence, waiting for me as I walked up the road from the school bus. She pranced back and forth as I got closer. Then we'd be off riding bareback over the hills. It was my favorite time of the day.

I liked to ride Buffy to the top of the hill behind our house. There I'd get off and watch her nibble at the grass and sniff the fresh air as I

DONNA RINE DEEM poses with Buffy and one of the 4-H trophies they won together.

sat on the ground beside her. She was my friend. I told her my thoughts and dreams and never had to worry that she would tell anyone my secrets.

It has been over 30 years since I lived on the farm, but I still think about those wonderful days. I occasionally get out my old photo albums, look at pictures of Buffy and feel like I'm still there with her on that hill in the pasture. ∩

Rebel Was in a Tornado— And Lived to Whinny About It

By Virginia Patrick, Tionesta, Pennsylvania

Forest County, Pennsylvania, where we live, is a sparsely populated rural county known for its abundance of trees and prime hunting and camping areas. Tornadoes were virtually unheard-of until May 31, 1985, when a devastating twister cut a mile-wide path through the middle of the county.

At the time, our son Jim was living in the homestead on German Hill, where I had grown up. That was the area hardest hit by the tornado.

When the storm hit, Jim headed for the basement. There wasn't time to get his dog, "Joe", or his horse, "Rebel", in from

Kendra Bond

the pasture behind the house. Within seconds, the house had completely blown off its foundation. Pieces were found a quarter of a mile away. The barn and doghouse were also gone. Jim escaped with only a few cuts and bruises, and Joe was unhurt, still tied to his stake in the yard. But Rebel was nowhere to be seen.

Jim discovered his brother, Rex, in the field near the spot where the house used to be. Rex was on his way to town and had pulled into Jim's yard just ahead of the storm. His car had overturned, and he had a broken arm and ankle.

Jim went for help, and when he returned, Rex told him he heard a horse whinny from across the road. Sure enough, there was Rebel working his way through twisted trees and debris. His ear was badly cut and he had some other scratches, but he was basically in good shape.

It was a miracle. As near as we can tell, Rebel was blown across the road by the storm—and lived to whinny about it. ∩

Someone Stole Her Horse!

By Kimbra Holmberg, Auburn, Washington

A horse was the only thing I ever begged my parents for …and I did a lot of begging! Secretly, I think Dad wanted a horse as much as I did. So when I was 13, Dad brought home "Nugget", a 4-year-old golden Palomino.

Not many of the girls I went to school with had horses, so I spent lots of time riding alone. But I didn't mind. Nugget and I had many adventures, including trying to outrun a Kansas hailstorm and a bumblebee.

When we moved from Wichita, Kansas to Monroe, Washington because of my father's job transfer, there was no way I was going to leave Nugget behind. At age 15, it was bad enough to leave treasured friends. So Dad bought a used horse trailer to move Nugget to our new home.

After I got married, my husband, Jon, and I moved to the foothills outside Seattle, where there were dairies and gen-

KIMBRA HOLMBERG and Nugget shared many adventures, including outrunning a hailstorm and escaping from a horse thief.

tlemen farmers. We rented a house on a lake acreage, where Nugget could roam with the landlord's three horses.

One bright May morning as I was heading to work, I found the gate into the property wide open. I'd heard some persistent whinnying during the early hours of the morning but hadn't thought much about it. However, when I didn't find any sign of the horses, I feared they had been stolen!

Hurried to the Auction

I frantically started making telephone calls and talked to the state branding inspector. He suggested that if we believed the horses had been stolen, we should go to the next livestock auction—just in case the thief was trying to sell them to make a quick buck.

There was a sale that day in Quincy, a 3-hour drive from where we lived. My dad went with me, and we arrived just before the sale was to begin. I hurried to where the sale animals were kept, and I found Nugget and my landlord's horses. I was seething with anger because not only had someone stolen my horse, he'd also cut Nugget's long and beautiful white mane and tail.

Dad and I notified the auction personnel, and a suspect was apprehended. I learned that he was released after only 1 night in jail, but at that point, I considered myself lucky just to get Nugget back. ∩

Two Horses Have a Special Place in Her Heart

By Karen Petersen, San Antonio, Texas

T he first horse I rode was an untrained white gelding named "Thunder".

It was during the summer before I started first grade, and my cousin Gary and I caught Thunder and tied a rope to his halter to make the reins. We fashioned a crude saddle from an old sack.

Near the end of the summer, Thunder spooked and I fell off—bottom first into a cactus. My parents were afraid I'd get hurt riding this untrained horse and got me a half horse/half pony named "Betsy". She was a brown and white Paint with one brown eye and one blue eye.

I wasn't very tall. So Dad showed me how to place the saddle on the fence, lead Betsy parallel to it, climb the fence and place the saddle on her. After that one lesson, Dad never helped me saddle Betsy again. I rode her every day.

One summer day, my two cousins and I were all riding Bet-

sy at the same time. We rode her into the pond so she could get a drink of water, just like we had seen on a television Western.

Dumped Them in the Mud

Well, Betsy was tired of carrying all of us at once. So when we got to the middle of the pond, she laid down and dumped the three of us into 2 feet of brown, sticky mud! We led her home and spent the afternoon cleaning mud off her, the saddle and ourselves.

When I was in fifth grade, Betsy unlatched her gate and got out. When Dad arrived home, he found her standing in the middle of the highway near our house. Betsy knew she was in trouble when she saw Dad and began to run. Her feet slipped on the pavement, and she fell hard. Dad got her to her pen, but she died from her injuries.

I was devastated, and while my parents felt sorry for me, they said, "No more horses!"

However, it wasn't long before I was back in the saddle again. The year after Betsy died, a friend moved to the city and needed someone to keep his horse, "Lady", until it was sold. He asked us since we had a nice corral and barn.

Parents Gave In

Lady was a Paint Quarter Horse mare, and I immediately fell in love with this beautiful animal. I pleaded with my parents, and they eventually gave in and bought her.

Lady was a wonderful horse, and I rode her almost every day for 15 years. I rode Western and English style, took her over homemade jumps, rode standing on her back and was even in a parade with her in downtown San Antonio. (Her only bad habit was taking my boyfriends under low tree limbs or dumping them over a fence!)

Everyone in the community knew Lady because of her distinctive coloring, and because I tied her on a long rope so she could eat grass near the road every day.

I continued riding Lady through college and after I was married. She lived a wonderful life and died at the ripe old age of 28—but not before my two daughters experienced the joy of riding her, too.

I've owned 10 horses over the years. But Lady and Betsy will always hold a special place in my heart. I'm thankful to have known them, cared for them and loved them. O

Horse Stayed Awake Thinking of Mischief

By Sally Kurtis, Niles, Michigan

My dreams came true in 1949 when my granddad gave me a 3-year-old bay filly. She was my first horse, and I named her "Ginger" after the character in the book *Black Beauty*.

I was young and inexperienced with horses, so Ginger taught me what I needed to know. I loved her dearly, even though some of those lessons were painful!

No one can tell me horses don't think. Ginger was smart, and I'm sure she stayed awake nights just thinking up mischievous things to do.

She could twist snaps open on tie-chains...get the tightest halter off...and open the sliding barn door with her teeth and squeeze through. I saw her roll under a one-strand electric fence to escape the pasture.

For fun, she would often lower her head into the water trough

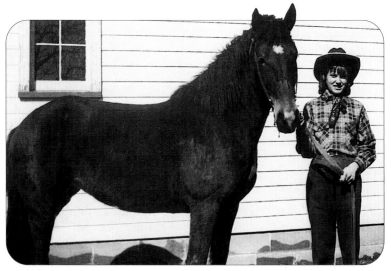

SALLY KURTIS received her first horse—this bay filly named Ginger—in 1949 from her grandfather.

up to her eyes and blow bubbles. Then she would fling her head up and splatter water all over anyone standing nearby.

Ginger was a "talking" horse, too. She'd greet us as we approached the barn and keep grunting and rumbling as long as we were around her. She also had strange taste buds. Tobacco and cheese sandwiches were among her favorites.

Ginger loved to run and was extremely fast, considering her stocky build. I found this out while riding with friends who tried to pass her.

Curiosity Got the Best of Her

She was hard to catch when she got loose, but her curiosity usually helped us capture her. She'd run away as soon as you got close to her. But if you picked something up, she'd want to know what it was and come right to you. Then we could take hold of her forelock and lead her with no problem.

I was lucky to have a horse, let alone a saddle. So for the first year, I rode bareback. One day I was riding home through a swamp, and the deer flies were biting her ears. She spun around and refused to go forward.

My dad happened to come along and slapped her on the rump. She jumped straight up and came down on stiff legs. The next thing I knew, I was lying on the ground with the breath knocked out of me.

I rode Ginger for 15 years, and it was a sad day when she died. She is buried in a field where we used to play. A piece of my heart lies there, too.

I'm glad to have memories of this little bay mare who brought so much happiness, love and, yes, exasperation into my life. Thanks, Granddad!

Houdini the Horse

By Athel McIntosh, Lebanon, Missouri

I once had a colt named "Sahara Zan" that was orphaned before he was a month old. So I raised him, first feeding him from a bottle.

We kept Sahara in a box stall, but every morning I took him

outside to brush and curry him. He loved it so much that when I finished one side, he immediately turned around so I could do the other side!

Soon he learned to open any doors and gates that weren't wired shut—and if he couldn't open them the easy way, he'd do it the hard way. We took Sahara over to our neighbor, Leroy, to be trained. One night Leroy's family heard a commotion in their yard. There was Sahara with the yard gate over his shoulders. He had stuck his head through the gate and lifted if off the hinges so he could go play with the kids.

We sold our farm and were getting ready to move. I had gone into the cellar room to pack when I heard clip-clop, clip-clop. I turned around and there was Sahara—in the house! He had opened the barn lot gate and the door to the house looking for me. That's when I decided I should have named him Houdini!

Palomino Pouts When She Doesn't Get Her Way

By Kimberly Anderson, Alma, Arkansas

When Dad and I began the search for my perfect horse, I knew it had to be gentle, loving and, most importantly, a beautiful golden Palomino.

We found bays, sorrels and horses of every other color imaginable—but not one Palomino. My father tried to convince me that the color didn't matter. But I stubbornly held on to my dream.

When I had just about given up hope, a local horse trader call Dad and told him he had a 3-year-old Palomino mare for sale. It was late in December, and he needed hay badly. So he was willing to trade the horse for hay.

I'll never forget the first moment I saw "China". She was as skinny as a rail with shaggy winter hair. But I instantly fell in love with her. Ten years and many miles later, she is a fat, sassy and beloved member of our family. And to think Dad tried to get me to settle for a bay or a sorrel!

China's most endearing trait is her tendency to pout when she doesn't get her way. Her lower lip quivers, and she gives me a look like "I am so unloved".

With a little extra attention and a handful of feed, I'm back in her good graces again. ◠

KIMBERLY ANDERSON refused to settle for any horse other than her beautiful Palomino. China has a personality all her own.

Buck Ate Her Cupcake

By Sis Robinson, Roxborough, Pennsylvania

My boyfriend, Al Robinson, gave me a buckskin named "Buck" for my 20th birthday, in 1941. That was before he knew he was going to be my husband! There were many trails throughout the Roxborough area of Pennsylvania, where we lived, and another leading to Valley Forge. So Al and I enjoyed spending our weekends riding the countryside.

We always took a saddlebag filled with a lunch, including chocolate cupcakes. One time while I was eating one, Buck came up, stuck his mouth in my hand and ate my cupcake! On every trip after that, I brought extra cupcakes for him.

There was a stable in the area with jumps, and although he was not too keen on it, I took Buck there to jump. One day

71

he refused to make the last jump.

He stopped dead in front of it, and I sailed over the fence and landed on the ground. Buck ran to the barn and jumped into a manure pile. I had quite a time walking him out of that mess.

That was the last time I put him through the jumps. He had made his feelings very clear to me.

In 1945, Al and I rented a house with a barn and bought more horses. I'd put our 2-year-old son in

front of me in the saddle and take him along on rides. When he grew up, he bought a farm and had horses of his own.

Now our granddaughter, Colleen, likes to ride. She even took her horse, "Rex", to college with her. It's a family joke that Rex went to college. ∩

SIS ROBINSON and her cow pony, Buck, enjoyed sleigh rides in the winter and trail rides during the rest of the year.

They Strapped a Crate to the Car And Hauled Their Pony Home

By Helen Rilling, Auburn, Illinois

I still nurse arthritis in the shoulder I broke 70 years ago, when I was thrown from a little Shetland pony named "Dixie". But the fond memories of that little pony make it all worthwhile.

We lived on a 400-acre grain farm in the central part of Illinois in the 1920s, and our family had gone to the state fair one day. About sundown, my father gathered my two sisters, my brother and me around him and announced that he had a surprise for us.

He loaded us into our new touring car, and we drove to the horse barns. There he introduced us to the most beautiful baby Shetland pony, about as big as a collie. Father carefully placed him in a crate and attached it to the running board of the car. We decided on his name on the way home.

We pampered Dixie and watched him grow. Finally Father pronounced that he was big enough to carry our weight. Eventually he became strong enough to carry all three of us girls at once.

Dixie was plump, and we seldom saddled him. We had to be careful when we did, because he learned to expand his belly when we tightened the cinch. Then when we stepped into the stirrups, we'd find the girth loose. The saddle would slip and toss us to the ground.

Dixie was smart in other ways, too. He learned to open barn doors and unlatch gates.

He Had a Mind of His Own

He also had a mind of his own. When we rode him down our long lane, he'd go as far as the gate and stop. No amount of coaxing would get him going, and we'd have to get off and lead him past the gate. Then he would continue on to the next gate, where he would balk again. It took a long time to ride to school some days!

Dixie and I were the "water boys" during the summer months. We carried jugs of fresh, cool water to the men plowing and planting the fields and to the threshing crews. Dixie

---

"No amount of coaxing would get Dixie going. We'd have to get off and lead him past the gate..."

---

was patient while the men drank, but he trotted faster and faster on the way back to the barn. This was the roughest ride you could ever imagine.

Tragedy struck when I was 12 years old. Rain ruined our crops, cholera killed the hogs, and with the Depression, Father couldn't pay his debts. So we had to sell everything, including Dixie, and move away.

A neighbor bought Dixie to use for riding out and getting his cows for milking, but Dixie didn't much like this arrangement. He had been boss for too long on our farm. The first time the neighbor rode him to fetch the cows, Dixie waded into the pond and lay down.

That's been many years ago. But the memories of Dixie are still as bright as his blue eyes. ∩

Barney Had More Smarts Than His Master

By Theodore Klassen, Abbotsford, British Columbia

Memories of my favorite horse go back to 1930, when my uncle gave me a gray mixed Shetland and Welsh pony named "Barney". He was just the right size for a 7-year-old boy, but he had more smarts than his supposed master.

The battle between Barney and me was on from the beginning. In fact, he threw me one of the first times I rode him, and I cracked my arm. I'm reminded of that to this day because my arm didn't heal correctly.

Technically, I rode Barney to school each day. However, in reality, it was simpler for me to just lead him the 1-1/2 miles. He had such a slow jarring walk that it took me longer to ride than to lead him. However, I could always count on a fast ride home!

One of his favorite tricks was to go through a clump of willow trees beside the road to see if he could unseat me. One time when we were out in the field rounding up the horses, he knocked me off by brushing me up against a fence post. I

> *"When Barney finally figured out I was the boss, we became good friends..."*

had to walk home with a bruised body and ego, and when my neighbor saw me, he wanted to know what the other fella looked like.

When Barney finally figured out I was the boss, we became good friends. He even learned several tricks that I liked. I'd lift up his left front foot, and he would lie down. Then I'd straddle him, and he'd get up with me on board.

I could also give him a little pinch and he would buck. We often did this to entertain people.

When I was chasing or herding cows, and one was not moving fast enough, I could touch Barney a certain way and he would nip the cow. Very effective! He got so he could move the herd almost by himself!

After we arrived at an understanding, it only took minutes to get to school. There was a small pasture attached to the school grounds for grazing in summer and a barn nearby for shelter in the winter. I rode Barney to school for 9 years.

It's too bad that all kids don't have the opportunity to match wits with an intelligent pet like my Barney. ∩

Warrior Was a Full-Size Horse on Pony Legs

By Vicki Hainey, Hannibal, New York

Of all the horses I have owned in the last 45 years, there's one that stands tall in my mind.

Back in the early 1970s, I was ready to graduate from a backyard horse to one I could compete with in the show ring. A trainer friend recommended a horse that he knew, and not long after that, "Lanark Warrior" came to live with my husband, me and our other horses.

Warrior was a full-size horse on pony legs, standing only 14.2 hands. His small stature, however, was deceiving. Anyone of any size could ride him and not look big.

Shortly after getting him, we took him to our first horse show. A friend and I rode Warrior all day and won every class we entered. We were ec-

WARRIOR turned out to be a horseman's dream, even though he had an attitude and a few bad habits.

static! Warrior turned out to be a horseman's dream. Even if we didn't ride him all week, we could still pull him out of the pasture on weekends and win at horse show competitions.

Warrior was not without his faults. He had an attitude that wouldn't quit, and he ate anything that wasn't tied down. His cribbing was so bad that he would chew on a rope or the edge of a trash can while we were waiting to go into the show ring. If he wasn't cribbing on trash cans, his head was buried over his ears in them looking for some goody to eat. Many unsuspecting people lost their hot dogs, bun and all, as they strolled by him at a show!

Warrior and I attended more horse shows over the years than I can count. We made friends and had lots of good times together. I will always be grateful for the "big horse in the little body".

      ☊

Bob Led the Funeral Procession To the Tavern

By Rev. William Dunstan, Randolph, Maine

My father was a country preacher, and in 1915, he went to his first parish, which consisted of three churches in western New York.

Of course, he had to have a horse, and he found a good-size but gentle mount called "Bob". Bob would plod along without guidance, except for turning. So my father would often lay down the reins and meditate or read.

One day Father was leading a funeral procession, and as usual, Bob had free rein. (My father said he was prayerfully meditating, but I suspect he was napping.) All of a sudden, Bob pricked up his ears, let out a whinny and swiftly trotted up to a roadside tavern! Luckily it had a circular drive, and my father was able to quickly ride out in front of the procession again.

He later found out that Bob had been owned by a farmer who took fresh produce into Buffalo. The farmer would leave

Bob Firth/Firth PhotoBank

before daylight, and the tavern was about halfway. So he'd stop there for breakfast and to feed the horse.

Father had an evening service about 3 miles from home. He'd ride Bob into the horse shed at the church and never bothered to tie him, since he always waited patiently. But Bob could apparently tell time. One Sunday evening my father preached a little longer than usual. When he finished, he discovered Bob had backed out of his stall and gone home. ◠

Buck Delivered Brother's Notes

By Minnie Thompson, Hoquiam, Washington

When my brother was 12, he was given an orphan buckskin Indian pony he called "Buck". My mother and brother raised him on a bottle.

When Buck was old enough to ride, my brother would take him to a friend's house, where the boys would make plans to go out.

My brother would write a note to our parents to tell them where he was going and stick it in the saddle. Then he'd slap Buck on the rump and say, "Go home, Buck." It wasn't long before Buck showed up at home with the note. ◠

The Girls Reminisce About the Family Pony

By Donna Nelson, Bridgeport, Nebraska

When my daughters were 12, 9, and 3, their grandpa showed up at our farm one day with a black Shetland pony. The pony had placed at the Wyoming State Fair pony competition, so Grandpa thought the girls could use him for their 4-H horse project. They named him "Blinkum".

The girls and I still reminisce about Blinkum when we get together. Janelle remembers her cousins from the city trying to ride him. He definitely had a mind of his own, and when he was tired, he'd go back to the corral—with the cousins sitting on his back crying because he wouldn't go where they wanted.

Kellee remembers the time she was out checking cows with Grandpa, and Blinkum accidentally bumped the electric fence. He became a racehorse very quickly! All she could do was hang on until he ran out of gas.

Lexie recalls riding too close to the barn gate. She caught her belt loop in the gate hook, and when Blinkum went into the corral, she was left hanging on the barn by her jeans.

My favorite memory of Blinkum was when we had to haul him somewhere. We didn't have a horse trailer, so we used the pickup with a stock rack. The end gate of the stock rack raised straight up, and you had to duck a little bit to get under it.

We would back the pickup into a depression to lower the rear. Blinkum never refused to load, but he had a ritual he did

---

*"**B**linkum would dance a little. Then all of a sudden he would leap like a rabbit into the pickup..."*

---

first. He'd dance a little with his front feet like he was getting ready—then all of a sudden he would leap like a rabbit into the pickup. It was hilarious to watch him. One time he jumped too high and conked his head on the bottom of the end gate. He made it in, but it jarred him. He stood there and shook his head as if to say, "What was that?"

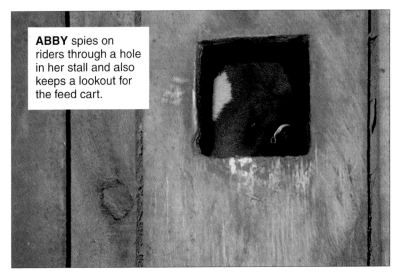

ABBY spies on riders through a hole in her stall and also keeps a lookout for the feed cart.

Riders Would Notice
An Eyeball Staring at Them

By Mary McIvor, Superior, Wisconsin

My horse Abby tends to be a social butterfly. She loves to know what is going on all around her.

The stable where I used to board her was a large facility, with two sections to the barn separated by an indoor riding arena. In the back of Abby's stall was a small square opening that looked into this riding arena. From there you could also see the entrance to the other side of the barn where the feed was kept.

During dinnertime, Abby would be on the watch. She would circle in her stall, stop by the opening and peer through it—circle and peer again. This would go on until she saw the feed cart come through the doorway and across the arena to her side of the barn. She would then make her "grumble-grumble" sound, and all the other horses knew chow was on the way.

Abby also liked to watch what was going on in the arena when people were riding. During clinics and lessons, she shocked riders when all of a sudden they'd notice an eyeball staring at them as they came down that side of the arena! ∩

MR. MR. was a beautiful horse with a white blaze down his face. He was a beauty on the inside, too.

Broken Leg Didn't Stop Her

By Sally Scott Salazar, Hayden, Colorado

My best friend for 4 years was a gelding the kids and I called "Mr. Mr." He was a beauty with a big white stripe down his face—that "one in a million" horse you always dream about.

I could put one of my 3-year-old twins on Mr. and never worry. He'd have followed me up a ladder if he could have when they were on him.

When I'd enter the barn, he would run and slide right up to me, whirl and run to the other side of the barn and then charge right back to me. When he stopped, he'd look at me as if to say, "How'd I do?"

I didn't know if anyone had ever ridden Mr. bareback before I had him, but one day I decided to give it a try. I had a badly broken leg, and the only exercise an old ranch girl like me knew was horseback riding. So I led Mr. beside the hay bunk in the barn and asked him to please not hurt me. I jumped on and had one of the best rides of my life.

My leg healed better and stronger than anyone had ever hoped. So after it mended, Mr. and I had a great time—jumping ditches, running through water and getting covered with mud. I felt like a kid again back on the farm.

Mr. was the most beautiful horse, inside and out, that I will ever have.

ᘯ

Red Belonged to Her Crush

By Marsha Allison, Montgomery, Alabama

Back in the 1970s, my dreams came true when my husband and I bought an older roping horse named "Red". He was a beautiful sorrel gelding about 16 hands high and gentle as a dove.

One of the reasons I fell in love with Red was because he belonged to a man I had a crush on when we were in school together. I'd gone to local rodeos to watch him rope. He was also an artist, and when he autographed my yearbook, he drew a horse with a rider holding a lasso in the air. He signed his name inside the lasso. (My husband was very understanding of this old high school crush!)

Gentle with Children

Red was so gentle that we didn't have to worry about him hurting our two boys, ages 3 and 6. He never moved a muscle when they were underfoot, and I do mean underfoot. They could literally walk under him, and he stood still as a statue.

Red was great for trail riding. He was so well trained as a roping horse, all I needed to do was lean a little, and he knew where I wanted to go.

He never ran me into brush or trees and wouldn't dream of knocking me off under a tree limb or stopping short at a creek to pitch me over his head. Children loved riding him, and we didn't mind sharing him.

The time came

Christopher Marona

when we had to give Red up because we needed to spend more time going to the children's ball games and shuffling them from place to place. It broke my heart, but we were lucky to find a teenage girl just learning to ride. She was a perfect match for our perfect horse.

His First Horse Was a Cow!

By John Paugstat, Georgetown, Kentucky

Being poor, we made do or we did without when I was growing up. So for a long time, the closest thing we had to a horse was a Guernsey cow named "Daisy".

We had the cow because Poppa believed what his poppa had taught him—a cow covers a lot of poverty. Daisy, true to form, provided us with milk and butter, and her calves provided meat. She also became my first "horse", which eventually led to my love for the real thing.

I wasn't old enough to be in school, but Poppa decided I was old enough to take care of Daisy. I wasn't thrilled with this awesome responsibility.

One day I was trying to move Daisy home from the pasture. She didn't want to go and showed her belligerence by switching her tail in my face. I grabbed the tail, and she started to run. I hung on and had one of my first "horse" experiences.

Felt Like He Was Flying

Daisy ran as fast as my little legs would move—then she ran faster! I hung on for dear life, and even though I wasn't actually riding Daisy, the evergreen trees breezed by me at speeds I had only imagined. After that, I was hooked on the notion of galloping through the countryside on a four-legged critter.

About that time, Poppa was able to buy a huge Belgian horse called "Tony". I could hardly wait to have Tony run with me on his back. But my challenge was to figure out how to get on top of this 6-foot, 2,000-pound monster.

One day I discovered Tony lying down. If I could just slowly sneak up and jump on his back, I thought.

This proved to be much easier said than done. Tony saw

JOHN PAUGSTAT has made friends with another horse. But his favorite mounts are a cow named Daisy and a draft horse named Tony.

me coming and off he went. If at first you don't succeed, try, try again. I did—again and again. Each time I learned a little and got closer. I was finally able to touch Tony before he stood up.

Crept Closer and Closer

After what seemed like an eternity, I found Tony lying down again one day. Slowly I inched my way toward him—pretending all the time to be totally disinterested in his siesta, but all the time praying he wouldn't get up.

Finally, I was close enough to touch Tony. I quickly jumped on his back and grabbed his mane. This startled Tony, and he jumped up almost as fast as I jumped on. Then he took off at a full gallop.

It was one of the most delightful rides of my life. Tony's gallop was so smooth, rhythmic and effortless. I knew this was Heaven. I could almost hear the angels sing! Unfortunately, I dropped out of Heaven and into the lap of Mother Nature when Tony decided to lower his head and raise his hind feet in a buck that threw me off faster than I'd jumped on!

I'm now in my mid-60s and have had some fantastic rides. However, none can match those given to me by my two favorite "horses", Daisy and Tony.   ∩

She and Foxy Covered Many Miles

By Mrs. Henry Roberts, Walla Walla, Washington

One of the reasons my childhood was so happy was my ornery lazy Pinto pony, "Foxy". We rode hundreds of miles together.

My cousin had been dragged by a horse when she caught her foot in a stirrup, so I wasn't allowed to have a saddle until we found one without stirrups. That was okay with me—I liked to ride bareback unless it was really hot.

That was the situation one summer when Foxy and I visited all the ranches for 20 miles around. I was selling subscriptions to the *Washington Farmer* paper in an effort to win a Shetland pony. The paper profited greatly from my efforts that hot summer, but I didn't win the pony.

Foxy would develop a terrible limp, especially when an adult rode him. But the minute his bridle was removed and he was turned loose in the barnyard, he would gaily gallop away with absolutely no sign of lameness.

Sometimes when we were on the way home from a ride, Foxy would "unload" me. Then he'd run ahead just out of reach, turning occasionally to give me a horselaugh.

"MY BEST FRIEND, Nora, and I were 10 when this picture was taken in 1917," writes Mrs. Henry Roberts.

I loved him dearly, and it was a sad day when I outgrew him and had to give him to a neighbor girl. I graduated to "Sally", a long-necked, long-legged bay mare whose sweet disposition and easy gait gave me many miles of wonderful riding.

Especially memorable to me are the evening rides we took under fantastic sunsets with the mournful cries of coyotes in the distance. But nothing quite compares to the miles I covered on Foxy.

Dunk in the River Taught Her To Trust Her Horse

By Donna Turner, Deer Park, Washington

In 1951, my family lived along the Spokane River on the Washington-Idaho border. I was 13 and had been riding since I was 7. My horse, "Shydonnie", was a solid bay gelding with a gentle disposition. He was half Tennessee walker and half Indian pony.

My little sister, Connie, who was 8 years old, had an Appaloosa/Shetland named "Doc". We spent countless hours exploring country trails on our horses. One day we were riding along the riverbank, when my friend Sylvia joined us on her Pinto pony. We decided to ride the horses into the water.

Connie couldn't swim, and Sylvia and I barely could. But Shydonnie was willing, so he and I were the first into the water. We made our way downstream to a tiny island, with Shydonnie and me on one side, and Sylvia and her pony on the other side of Doc and Connie —just in case they ran into trouble with a strong current.

DONNA TURNER proudly shows off Shydonnie (above) while sister Connie sits astride Doc (below).

We repeated this trip several times before deciding to ride farther upriver so we could have a longer swim back. This time Shydonnie did not want go into the river. I swatted him with the reins to finally coax him in.

Almost immediately Shydonnie fell into a large underwater hole and began lunging to get out. I knew you could drown a horse by pulling on the reins. So I threw the reins outward and grabbed his neck as my body floated off him.

Shydonnie lunged and lunged and finally got us out of the hole. Our swim was over.

I learned two important lessons that day. First, swimming the river is a really stu-

pid thing to do. Second, if you have a horse you really trust, watch and listen to him.

Connie eventually fell heir to Shydonnie. She gamed on him, and in 1960, they won Reserve Championship in the Washington Barrel Racing Association. They set one record that stood for 17 years.

Shydonnie was quite a horse.   ∩

Daisy Was Smarter Than the Average Horse

By Vera Easton, Bismarck, North Dakota

I'm 100 years old. Now that it's the year 2000, I have lived in three centuries!

I had a horse named "Daisy" that was my transportation from about 1920 to 1934. She was a smart horse and understood me when I talked to her.

I'm not just talking about "whoa" and "giddap". All horses know that. She knew a lot more. If I said, "Back, Daisy," she would take a backward step. Once I walked into her stall, and she stepped on my foot. I said, "Daisy, you're on my foot." She quickly lifted her hoof and never stepped on me again.

One day we were driving some cattle into the yard. While chasing a cow, we ran into some barbed wire laying on the ground. The wire wrapped around Daisy's front foot and threw her down hard. I flew off unhurt.

I petted Daisy and told her not to struggle. She immediately lay still, while I got an ax from the woodpile to cut the wire and unwind it from her leg.

Then I laid my hand on her neck and asked her to get up. She stood right up—luckily not seriously hurt.

I herded sheep with Daisy, too. On hot days, I'd position Daisy so she cast a shadow big enough for me to sit in. She wouldn't move as long as I was sitting on the ground beside her. By noon, the shadow would be so small that I was almost under her. But she never stepped on me.   ∩

Wild Horse Could Be Gentle When He Needed to Be

By Ernest Vining, Prescott Valley, Arizona

I grew up on a 640-acre farm in southeast Kansas. My older brother, Jess, traded for a saddle horse named "Dan". He was a beautiful animal, but quite wild.

When Jess or I would climb on, Dan was off and running. That was fine with us, but we were worried about our father, whose hands and feet were crippled.

It wasn't long before Dad wanted to go someplace and needed to ride Dan. We saddled him, then stood on both sides of his head and held on to the bridle while Dad slowly pulled himself up into the saddle.

When Dad was ready, we apprehensively let go of the bridle and stepped aside. We could not believe it. Dan stood perfectly still until Dad said, "Okay, Dan. Let's go."

Dan started walking along like an old plow horse, while Jess and I just shook out heads. When Dad got home, Jess took the reins and climbed on. Dan was off like greased lightning!

One of my chores was to bring the cows in from the pasture at milking time. One evening I rode Dan bareback and de-

> **"Jess and I just shook our heads when wild Dan started walking like an old plow horse..."**

cided to throw my right leg over his withers and ride sidesaddle. Just then a rabbit jumped out of the bushes. Dan shied to the left and I fell off, hitting the ground and breaking my shoulder.

I was sitting on the ground moaning, when Dan came over and nudged me several times as if to say, "I'm sorry, Ernie." When I didn't get up, he took off for the house and nickered up a storm until Jess came.

When Jess saw Dan, but no cows and no Ernie, he knew something was wrong. He jumped on Dan's back, and Dan took him right back to me. We decided then and there that Dan was a very special horse.

"EVERYTHING I NEEDED to know about life, I learned from Scout, my horse and good friend," says Debbie Sears.

They Reached a Compromise About Jumping Fences

By Debbie Sears, St. Charles, Illinois

I was horse crazy by the time I was 8 years old and begged my parents for riding lessons. Finally, when I was 13, they gave in, although Dad was convinced I'd take a couple lessons and lose interest. I set out to prove him wrong.

I had a wonderful instructor, Harold, at a local stable who not only taught me to ride, but more importantly, taught me the importance of taking care of the animals that gave me so much pleasure. When it came to grooming, he explained that I needed to spend as much time off my horse as I did on him. Grooming before and after I rode was essential. There was no compromise in this area.

"Scout" was one of the "school" horses at the stable. The first time I saw him, I thought he was sweet but a little homely. He was also a little green, but so was I. Harold thought it would be good if we learned together, and so the adventure began.

I was learning to jump and loved every minute of it. So Harold mounted me on Scout to see how we'd do together.

Things were going well during the lesson until the jumping

started. To put it simply, Scout and I compromised that day. I wanted to jump over the fence, and he didn't—so I went over the fence, and he didn't! It was the beginning of a long and happy friendship.

Graduation Gift

I rode and showed Scout all through my high school years. When graduation day came, my parents surprised me and bought Scout for me as a graduation present. It was the happiest day of my life.

The riding stable was sold, and I needed to find a new place to board Scout. I found a private farm that was perfect—it had a riding ring, lots of pastures and trails and a big pond that was great for swimming. I'd always wanted to take Scout swimming but never had a place to do it.

On a hot July day, I jumped on Scout bareback and headed for the pond. In we went, going deeper and deeper toward the middle. All of a sudden, I was floating in the pond without a horse under me. Scout had totally disappeared. My first thought was how I was going to get Scout out of the water and perform CPR on him.

But before I had time to panic, Scout was back underneath me, blowing water out of his nose and paddling around. Then he was gone again! He paddled around some more, then dove under again. My crazy horse was doing this on purpose—he liked diving under water!

Scout and I spent many happy years together. When I got married, Scout came with me. He even learned to like my husband!

Two for the Price of One

By Juli Jayne, Fairport, New York

When I graduated from college in 1967, I had two ambitions: to begin using my teaching degree and to buy a horse.

I was hired to teach first grade—at the whopping salary of $5,900—and immediately started looking for my dream

horse. I found a 3-year-old Appaloosa mare named "Shali-mar" that had recently been shipped in from Oklahoma.

Shalimar was mostly white with large black spots on her rump and a mottling of spots over the rest of her body. With youthful confidence and inexperience, I purchased her on the spot. On the way home, I realized I had no place to keep a horse. Luckily I found one only 3 miles from where I lived.

Each morning I got up at 6 a.m., walked to the barn and fed Shalimar. After chores, I returned home, changed clothes, walked to school and taught until 2:15 p.m. Then I repeated the whole business.

I bought a used English saddle and bridle so we could ride, but the most fun was caring for Shalimar and getting to know her. She knew my schedule and waited for me to feed and play with her.

I thought Shalimar was beautiful and would throw won-derful colts, so I started reading everything I could about breeding and foaling. Then I set up an appointment with my vet to have Shalimar checked before having her bred to a nearby Appaloosa stallion.

Mares carry their foals for approximately 11 months, so I

94

figured I had plenty of time to plan for the arrival of a new baby. Imagine my surprise when the vet told me Shalimar was already bred and due to foal soon.

By this time, I had become engaged to a fellow teacher. He didn't have a horse, but he did drive a '67 Mustang!

That night, we drove out to check on Shalimar. As we pulled into the driveway, we found her standing under a cherry tree in the pasture with a brand-new foal lying on the ground beside her. She had delivered a full-term spotted stud colt which, under the circumstances, we christened "Early".

Shalimar and Early were the beginning of my 30-year love affair with horses. I have fond memories of my first horse and her unexpected foal, but I think my husband would rather have his '67 Mustang convertible back! ∩

Future President Joined Their Ride

By Delphine Smith, Bloomington, Indiana

Back in the 1940s, Dad owned a riding stable in Ottawa, Illinois. We went on a lot of trail rides following a path along the old Illinois-Michigan Canal. I always rode my

gentle horse, "Jerry".

One day Dad told me an actor from Dixon, Illinois was going to join our ride. There were over 100 riders on the trail that day, and future President Ronald Reagan was among them. ∩

DELPHINE SMITH and Jerry escorted hundreds of trail riders at her father's stable in Illinois.

95

Sissy Was Spirited But Sweet

By Jill Leebrick, Milwaukie, Oregon

D ad bought "Sissy" when she was 16 years old. At that age and with a name like Sissy, I figured she'd be a calm and gentle horse. What I didn't know was that she had been used for gaming—like barrel racing and pole bending. She was spirited with a capital "S".

Dad belonged to a mounted posse that would get together and play polo. Sissy was perfect for this. You'd never believe she was 16 when you watched her play. When Dad finished a game, he'd ask me to cool her off. There was no way I was ever going to get on her back, so I'd just lead her around until she was dry. Even that made me nervous.

I preferred Dad's other horse because he was calm and safe—even though he was an uncomfortable ride. I always had a sore back after I rode him, but that was okay. I was not going to ride Sissy.

Several years later, Mom and Dad moved out of town, and I rented their house until it was sold. Dad also left Sissy for me to take care of and exercise.

Listened to Her Problems

I eventually got tired of walking her for miles. I decided it was crazy for both of us to work so hard, so I started riding her. I even started to trust her…and was surprised at how smooth and comfortable she was to ride.

We'd ride for hours. She heard all my problems and listened to my bad singing—with no complaints! I was beginning to fall in love with this horse.

The real clincher was when I was riding her toward home one day. She was always eager to get back to the barn, and I was holding her back at a trot when she tripped in a hole. She went down, and I fell off.

I just knew she was going to race to the barn about a mile away and I'd have to hike back. But I looked up to find her standing right next to me. She had a concerned look as if to say, "Are you all right?"

That was the turning point in our relationship. That horse

had the biggest heart. I was amazed at how loving and affectionate she was to me after we got to know one another. She was nothing like the crazy, unpredictable and spirited animal I thought she was.

Eventually I even did some gaming on Sissy. I didn't have to know what I was doing—I just held on. She was such a pro I think she could have gone around those barrels blindfolded. I had never had so much fun.

Thanks, Sissy! Thanks, Dad!

Sonny Loved to Have His Hair Done

By Gidget King, St. Francis, Kansas

I once owned a wonderful Palomino named "Sonny". I broke him when he was 3 and boarded him at the fairgrounds where I trained horses.

Sonny was the talk of the fairgrounds. No matter what job had to be done, he was always in a good mood and happy to do anything I asked—whether it was moving calves, exercising young colts or riding muddy alleys.

When Sonny wasn't working, he acted like a kid. He pulled pranks on the horses in neighboring stalls...and he loved to have his hair done! ∩

SONNY seemed more than happy to oblige the camera with a close-up pose. And why not—he'd just been primped.

This Horse Could Count!

By B.F. Pennock, Cottonwood, Arizona

When I was a lad of 15, my closest friend owned a 3-year-old bay stallion named "Tony". He taught Tony a few tricks, including striking the ground three times with his hoof when you asked him how old he was.

When my friend had to move out of state, he sold Tony to me. I had a great time racing Tony against my brother's horse.

But eventually I reached an age when I needed a team more than a saddle horse. So I traded Tony for a pair of mules I could use to make my living.

Years later, I saw a man plowing a field with a pair of bay horses. One looked familiar, and upon investigation, I learned that it was Tony.

The owner asked me if I knew how old Tony was. I grabbed Tony's bits and rubbed his nose a little—then asked him how old he was. He struck the ground three times!

Of course, by then Tony was actually 13. So I told the owner he just forgot to add a digit. ∩

Texas Rangers Halted Their Ride to School

By Josephine Campion DeLany, Seguin, Texas

JOSEPHINE CAMPION DELANY
got Dan in a swap for a yearling bull.

When I was 10, we lived on a ranch that joined some thick, hilly woods between two counties. This area was called the Boundary. There were a lot of horses, some cattle and even a few wild hogs in there. Some of the horses and cattle were branded, some were not.

A tall skinny bay came out of the Boundary and began hanging around our work-horses at the barn. I petted and fed him, and when no one was watching, I'd climb on his back and go for a ride. I loved that horse and prayed every night that I could own him someday.

One day a man came riding by leading the bay. He told Dad he was an orphan that had lost his mother in a forest fire. He said he didn't want him and offered to sell him to Dad for $25.

Daddy offered to trade a yearling bull. I was listening, but not breathing. When the man said, "Sold," I ran and got the bridle I had kept hidden. I slipped it on the bay and rode him into the yard. Daddy grinned at Mama and said, "Looks like something's been going on!"

I named my horse "Dan" and rode him to grade school every year—and then to high school. The round-trip to high school was about 15 miles through a river and across two ranches. Sometimes the river would be on the rise and Dan would have to swim.

One morning in May 1934, I was running late for school.

Dan and I were really moving when we burst out of the brush and almost crashed into a big black sedan parked along the road. There were three men holding rifles and armed with pistols standing by the car. From Dan's back, I could see a machine gun on the backseat.

The men were dressed in dark clothing and wore black leggings and black hats. They were as startled as I was. They searched my leather schoolbag, looked at my books and then let me go.

I later found out they were Texas Rangers hunting Bonnie Parker and Clyde Barrow, the notorious bank robbers. I had long reddish hair and a freckled nose like Bonnie Parker, so no wonder they searched me.

Dan lived to be 30 years old. Four of my children learned to ride on him. My youngest son was born after Dan died. I named him Dan after the best horse that ever lived. ∩

Prince Willy Saved Boy's Life

By David Howell, Enon Valley, Pennsylvania

I bought "Willy" when I was about 10 with money I made selling *TV Guide* magazines.

Every Saturday, I traveled my 21-mile route on my bike. Between two of the villages on the route was a small farm on top of a steep hill. There was a shaggy brown horse in the pasture, and every time I came by, he trotted up to the fence. I was convinced he was waiting for me every Saturday.

We boarded horses at our farm, and I had plenty of nice ones to ride whenever I wanted. But I wanted one of my very own, so I bought Willy.

Willy's stomach rumbled whenever he cantered, his shaggy hair didn't shed until October, he was balky, stubborn—and nervous at times because he had only one good eye. But he was mine and I loved him.

Willy and I enjoyed exploring the vast countryside behind our small farm in western Pennsylvania. On warm summer evenings, I would look for him in the wooded pasture, climb on and lay down on his shaggy back with my ankles crossed over his neck. He would continue to graze with the other horses, but he'd walk so carefully that even if I dozed off, he didn't let me fall. This practice is probably what saved my life.

One hot summer day, Willy and I rode, as we often did, to a swimming hole in an abandoned strip mine several miles from home. I had light blond hair and fair skin, and on this particular day, I must have been in the hot sun too long. Willy was in the water with me when I began to get dizzy. My head was crackling, and I felt faint. I pulled myself onto his back and the last thing I remember was whispering, "Willy, go home."

When I woke up, I was packed in ice on the couch in our home. My family was gathered around me, and my mother was praying.

Dad told me later they had been in the kitchen, when he happened to look outside. Willy was standing just outside the door, with me draped unconscious across his back.

Willy never walked up to the house when we came back from riding. He always stubbornly tried to go straight to the barn. If I wanted him to keep going, there was a clash of wills. But not this day. Somehow he knew exactly what he had to do.

After that day, he was always known as Prince Willy!

Perfect Pony for A Dozen Ornery Kids

By Dorothy Gray, Romulus, Michigan

During the 1940s and '50s, we lived in Royal, Iowa. There were 12 of us kids, eight girls and four boys, and one day Dad came home with a Shetland pony we decided to call "Nibbs".

There were five or six of us going to school all of the time. So Dad made a pony cart and, weather permitting, Nibbs took us to our one-room school about a mile away.

Our favorite thing to do was to line Nibbs up along our

clothesline so all 12 of us could hang onto the line and try to climb on Nibbs. Sometimes (when Dad wasn't around) we'd open the back doors to the car and lead Nibbs through.

One day when Mom and Dad were gone, we even took Nibbs up on the back porch and into the kitchen. We got him out in a hurry when we saw the folks coming home.

Nibbs could get into trouble on his own, too. He learned to unlatch some of the barn doors and get into the feed bins.

Nibbs was the greatest little pony ever. He was kind and gentle—he had to be around the 12 of us! ∩

Babe Needed to Wash Behind Her Ears Before School

By Ola Brown, Mooresville, Indiana

In 1924, there were two ways to get to school—walk or ride horseback. I rode a horse named "Babe" and put her in an old livery stable while I was in class.

I'm almost 90, but I still recall the day I tried to saddle Babe, and she decided to roll on the ground. It had been raining and was very muddy. She was quite a sight when I got to school with mud caked all over her. My friends thought it was pretty funny! ∩

BABE IS LED by Ola Brown's father, Alfred, while her daughter Pat takes a ride.

POSING FOR THE CAMERA was old hat for a star like Clyde, shown here with owner Jim Brown.

Clyde Was a TV Star

By Jim Brown, Merrill, Wisconsin

When I lived in Canyon Country, California, I bought a lame Palomino named "Clyde". Fortunately the lameness was caused by a stone imbedded in his hoof. Once the stone was removed, the lameness left.

While I was building a canopy over a feeding area in our corral, Clyde kept knocking over the stepladder I was using. This continued until it became a neighborhood joke.

Clyde had been trained to perform on the TV series *Lassie*, and one day a neighborhood boy told me he knew why Clyde was knocking over the ladder. The boy had been watching a Lassie rerun. He saw Clyde knocking over a ladder with a pail of water on it so it would put out a fire that had been started by a match carelessly discarded in some straw. ◠

If It's Meant to Be, It Will Be

By Cindy Coatney, Southport, Florida

Thirteen years ago, we moved to the country so my husband could have a place to hunt and I could eventually get a horse. But I became busy with household chores and babies, and there was no time to think about my little dream.

Two years ago, I decided it was time to start looking for the horse I had longed for. I asked a friend who works at a local feed store to keep her eyes open for a young, inexpensive horse—one I could gently break by myself.

The following week, she brought me a picture of a horse. I immediately fell in love and knew this was the horse I had been waiting for. I called and made an appointment for the next day.

When we pulled up to see the horse, there was another family there to look at him, too! I couldn't believe it. How could someone else be looking at *my* horse? Just 2 hours earlier, I had confirmed our appointment.

We all went to take a look. He was at the far end of his pasture when he spotted us and came running as fast as he could to where we were standing. He was so beautiful with his head held high, ears alert and tail raised.

CINDY COATNEY fell in love with Diamond Jubilee the minute she saw his picture.

The next thing I knew, the other couple was writing out a check for him. I cried all the way home, but I finally decided God must not have wanted me to have this horse and that another would come along.

A month later, I saw the man who beat me to the punch in town. I asked him how the horse was. He told me he was very aggressive, had some bad habits and was not working out as they'd hoped.

I figured all this 17-month-old colt needed was just a lot of attention. So I asked if he'd consider selling him to me. I couldn't believe my ears when he agreed.

All He Needed Was Love

We decided to look at him the very next day. What we found made me cry all over again. He was in a pen that was covered with oil and auto parts, with another horse that was skin and bones and not happy about sharing his space. He had bite marks all over his flanks and a large knot in his mane. Worst of all, his beautiful eyes had no sparkle—no life in them.

We left and went immediately to buy fencing materials. We took them home and worked all day putting up a corral. We borrowed a trailer from a neighbor and went and got the horse before dark. I didn't want him to spend another night in those horrible conditions.

We named my new horse "Diamond Jubilee" because of the perfectly shaped diamond on his forehead.

Diamond Jubilee has now been with us for 1-1/2 years and has been a wonderful addition to our family. He has never shown any bad habits—besides chasing dogs. When the time came, I was able to saddle and ride him without any problem.

Each day I think how lucky I am to have him—and how important it is to be patient. If it is meant to be, it will be! ⌒

Ugly Horse Won Her Heart

By Tracey Belshee, Monroe, Oregon

An ugly horse named "Flash" taught me a lesson in humility and that beauty is more than skin-deep. My husband, Don, had bought me a beautiful mare that I'd taken to a stable for a couple months of training. She was one of those "push button" horses—an experienced horse that took care of business in the show ring and was a pleasure to ride. But she lacked in the personality department.

One day as I strolled down the alleyway of the barn while the trainer was putting my mare through her paces, I saw Flash

FLASH has a charming personality that makes him beautiful to everyone who gets to know him.

for the very first time. He was a blue-eyed 2-year-old Paint gelding that stood about 15 hands tall.

His thick bright white winter coat made him look like a polar bear. He had one brown ear, two brown spots on his belly and a small streak of black hair that ran through his forelock and tail.

What a sight! Who would want to buy an ugly horse like that, I thought.

As the days passed, I noticed how Flash would come to the stall door when people passed by. He was always receptive to visitors, and even though he was largely untrained, riders of all experience levels could handle him. I never saw him buck or try anything with a rider.

Only a Loaner

One day I was at a horse show in Eugene, Oregon. During a Western pleasure class, for some unexplainable reason, my mare stopped and refused to go forward. She threw a fit. I was disappointed and embarrassed when I had to get off and walk her out of the ring.

I was suppose to take her home with me, but my trainer suggested I leave her at the stable for more work. She said I could take Flash home so I'd have a horse to ride. Reluctantly I agreed.

When I got home with Flash that night, Don came out to greet me. He got within 20 feet of the trailer and stopped dead in his tracks. "What is that?" he asked as Flash peered through a window of the trailer. "He's only a loaner," I promised.

Flash became the talk of the neighborhood over the next

couple of weeks. His ugly looks caught everyone's eye, but his personality and calm demeanor intrigued them.

He passed the most important test when he charmed Don. Flash found it entertaining to sneak up on him and gingerly remove his baseball cap with his teeth. Then he'd wave it in the air as if to say, "Look what I have."

Wanted to Buy Him

The first day I took Flash for a trail ride, my neighbor asked me if I wanted to sell him. He was amazed how an untrained 2-year-old could behave so well.

Of course, Flash wasn't mine to sell at that point in time. But when my trainer decided to sell some of her stock, she thought I was crazy when I told her I wanted him.

In the months that followed, Flash was shown at various schooling shows by riders of all age groups. He may not have won every event he was entered in, but he won the hearts of every child and adult who came to know and ride him.

I guess the thing I like best about Flash is that he makes me laugh. He's always at the fence to greet me when my car pulls into the driveway. I think if he could reach his bridle, he'd put it on himself just so we could go for a ride.

Today Flash and I ride the hills around our home. His show career is on temporary hold so he can just be my horse. ◠

Mustang Won the Race by 50 Yards

By Art Bundy, Wilson, North Carolina

I was 10 years old in 1932 when my dad bought a couple of 2-year-old part-mustangs from Wyoming. My favorite was a strawberry roan filly Dad named "Flora". I thought she was beautiful, but she was as wild and tough as they come.

We farmed in eastern Nebraska near the Platte River. Dad bought these horses because they were supposed to be good cattle horses and because they were cheap in the middle of the Great Depression.

Dad and my 18-year-old brother, John, normally broke our

horses. John tried to saddle Flora and mount her, but she was so wild that Dad couldn't hold her. So John gave up in disgust.

It was my job to bring in the milk cows from the pasture

"On the sly, I started feeding her with a little alfalfa for dessert..."

---

and the stocker cattle that gleaned the fields in early winter. I rode "Dan", Dad's old horse, but he'd bite me every chance he got.

I wanted Flora, so on the sly, I started petting her and giving her apples and cow feed with a little alfalfa hay for dessert. Within a month, I could curry her and walk around her. By summer, I could bridle her, saddle her and walk her in the alley behind the stalls.

By early fall, I'd take Flora out behind the barn and ride her. Then Dad caught me riding her one day. He gave me a lecture about sneaking around behind his back. "What if you'd gotten hurt?" he asked.

I begged Dad to let me ride Flora around the barn while he watched. He agreed, and Flora and I did well—so well that he allowed me to keep training her. By early winter, Flora and I

FLORA RELUCTANTLY POSED for this picture in 1939 with Art Bundy's brother Bob. "She was a one-man horse," writes Art. "Notice her laid-back ears!"

were bringing in the stocker calves every day.

Flora had the smoothest ride of any horse I have ever ridden. She learned to neck rein and come to a sliding stop. She had the most "bottom" (wind) of any horse I've ever seen and could handle rough terrain on a dead run.

Flora also outran every horse in the area. One fellow came 8 miles to challenge us to a race one Sunday. In a mile-long race, Flora beat his horse by over 50 yards!

The Depression years were difficult, but having Flora as my best friend made them a lot easier to bear. I've owned some high-priced Quarter Horses during my lifetime, but Flora is the one horse I'll never forget.

Yikes! Bumblebees!

By Carol Scaggs, Highland, Illinois

My horse "Miggy" is a gray Arabian. As a young horse, she was pretty spirited. But as time passed, she seasoned out and is now a good horse for our granddaughters to ride.

When our granddaughter Felicia was about 9 and had been riding for a couple of years, my husband, Ron, and I took her

MIGGY and Felicia, Carol Scaggs' granddaughter, have become trail partners.

trail riding with us. We tacked up our three horses and set out on a beautiful trail. I was in the lead, Felicia was second and Ron brought up the rear.

We had been out on the trail for about 2 hours and were crossing a dry creek bed when we stirred up an angry swarm of ground bees. I was safely past the bees when they attacked. But they were angrily stinging Miggy, and she was dancing frantically.

We yelled to Felicia to kick Miggy and to run out of there! Finally Felicia got the message, and we all took off.

About a quarter mile down the trail, Felicia, saddle and all, fell off Miggy. Fortunately, Felicia was not scared or hurt. And we all breathed a sigh of relief.

The saddle she was using was the pony saddle, which had a very short girth strap. All that time Miggy was being stung, she was heaving deep breaths—loosening the short girth strap to the point that the saddle eventually fell off. We looked at each other and offered a prayer of thanksgiving that the saddle hadn't fallen off during the bee attack.　　　　Ω

Little Cow Pony Made Cattle Chores a Breeze

By Dale Hughes, Bakersfield, California

Our family moved to a farm in southwest Oklahoma in 1934, when I was 9. We were a large family, eight children plus Mom and Dad. Dad grew cotton, wheat and oats. We also raised chickens, hogs and had a small herd of milk cows.

One of my chores was to round up the dairy cows on foot in the afternoon and herd them to the barn for milking. They always seemed to be at the very back of the pasture when it was time for them to come in. But at least they stayed in the barnyard overnight to be milked in the morning.

As our dairy grew, the pasture on the home place could no longer sustain the cows and our two teams of workhorses. So

Dusty L. Perin

Dad leased extra pasture nearly a mile away. That was a long way to drive the cows on foot, so Dad went to an auction and brought home a small bay-colored horse we called "Peanuts". He became my horse because I was the one who always had to get the cows.

Was I ever in for a pleasant surprise! On my first ride down the dirt road to the pasture, Peanuts struck a gait that was smooth as silk. There was no jostling up and down whatsoever.

Bob Firth/Firth PhotoBank

When we arrived at the pasture gate, I opened it and Peanuts did the rest. Turns out he was a professionally trained cow pony. He took it upon himself to round up the cattle, drive them to the gate and up the road to the barn. If a cow lingered too long to graze, he'd nip her on the rump to get her to stay with the herd.

The Depression and Dust Bowl conditions caught up with us, and we had to sell out and move from the farm in 1939. It's been nearly 60 years since I've been on a horse. But I'll never forget Peanuts.

"**J.D.** watched over me and was the best friend I ever had," says Marc Dingfelder.

J.D. Didn't Hold a Grudge

By Marc Dingfelder, Warsaw, Missouri

Many years ago, I had a horse named "J.D." that I was particularly fond of.

We didn't have a stock trailer, so I hauled him around in the back of a pickup when working cattle. All I had to do was say, "J.D., load up!" and the horse would jump into the back of the pickup. To unload, I simply said, "Get out!"

I worked for a rancher named Frank, who was impressed with J.D.'s ability to listen. He hauled all of the horses to the pasture one day in his horse trailer, and after working cattle for a while, we took a break and were sitting around while the horses grazed.

Frank leaned over to another cowboy and said, "Watch this." Then, he hollered, "J.D., load up." J.D. walked around to the back of the trailer and stood there nervously shifting his weight from side to side. We couldn't see the back of the trailer—just that J.D. was nervously dancing about.

Again, Frank yelled, "Load up!" J.D. continued to shift his weight back and forth, only a little faster.

Frank yelled a third time, "Load up!" Then we heard a loud clunk. We went to the rear of the trailer and discovered the end gate was closed...but poor J.D. had tried to load up anyway and banged his head on the closed gate. He stood there staring at us as if we were nuts and couldn't believe we asked him to do that.

J.D. didn't hold a grudge, however. Good thing, because while working cattle in Florida some time later, I roped a Brahman calf to doctor it. The calf was bawling and making a fuss, but his mother didn't appear to be anywhere around.

Just as I finished putting medicine on the calf, I heard the mama cow charging toward us. I didn't have time to get back on J.D. So I grabbed his reins and pulled him in front of me —figuring he could take the hit from the charging cow better than I could.

At that instant, J.D. swung his rear around and began beating a tattoo on the mother cow with his hooves. He wouldn't let her anywhere near me.

From that day on, J.D. watched over me and kept the cattle away every time I dismounted. He was the best friend I have ever had.   ∩

This Kid Had a Mind of His Own

By Carl Sanda, Williston, North Dakota

I'll never forget a chestnut horse named "Kid" that we had while I was growing up on the farm. This horse definitely had a mind of his own.

He could open any door in the barn, and at times, he even unlatched the door of the feed bin. When he was hitched to a wagon, he often walked into the slough and laid down, refusing to move until he was unhitched. Then he'd get up and walk home. He would do the same thing if I was riding him, and he dumped me into the water more times than I'd care to admit.

I often rode Kid to visit a neighbor and tied him up near the water tank. Somehow, he'd get loose and would be wandering around the yard when I was ready to go home.

Problem was, he'd never let me catch him. He'd start for home, walking just out of my reach ahead of me. If I ran, he ran. If I stopped, he stopped. He'd look around at me once in a while, and I'm convinced he was laughing as I followed him all the way home.

Then came a day I will always remember. I was 16 and riding Kid for the spring horse roundup. We were galloping over rough ground, when he stumbled and fell. I fell off and Kid rolled over me.

He got up and trotted off. I lay there stunned and in pain. I could feel the sharp edges of broken ribs in my side.

Out of the corner of my eye, I saw Kid standing at the top of the hill looking at me. After a few moments, he came down and stopped by me. He waited while I grabbed his mane and painfully pulled myself onto his back. Then Kid, walking slowly and carefully, carried me home. ∩

Jake Was a Great Teacher

By Megan Darnell, Newcastle, Wyoming

When I was 3, "Jake" seemed like the biggest horse in the world to me—even though Dad said he was actually only 14-1/2 hands tall.

He was also the most beautiful animal I'd ever seen. His coat was a dark bay color, with a flowing black mane and tail and a full white blaze on his face.

Jake taught me many lessons about life—like how to trust. I was so small when I first started riding that wherever Jake wanted to go, I went, too. When we were moving cattle, Dad would leave me and Jake alone to follow behind the herd. Every now and then, Dad would come back to check on us, but we were always okay. I knew Jake would take care of me.

I also learned how to be a good friend from Jake. Every day when I came home from school, he was there to listen to my stories. He would see things from my point of view. And if I was feeling down, he looked at me with his large liquid eyes and assured me that things would be all right.

But probably the most difficult lesson he taught me was

JAKE was only 14-1/2 hands tall, but he looked like a giant to 3-1/2-year-old Megan Darnell when this photo was taken in 1983.

persistence—that no matter what goes wrong, I have to get back on and ride.

I was 7 years old when I rode in my first junior rodeo. I watched in amazement as the older girls whirled around the barrels on horseback. One girl didn't even hold onto the saddle horn. She was my idol.

The announcer called my name, and Jake and I took our turn at the barrel race. The wind whistled around my face, and I believed Jake was going to win.

Around the first barrel we flew. Emulating my idol, I wasn't hanging on, and suddenly I was on the ground looking up at Jake's hooves. He stumbled and almost fell as he avoided stepping on me. I climbed back on Jake and finished my barrel pattern. But the only thing we won that day was the Hardluck Cowgirl Buckle.

By the time I was in fifth grade, I was too big to ride Jake. I got a new, younger horse to ride.

Meanwhile, my young cousin, Cameron, was old enough for his first horse. So on a sunny Easter Sunday, I sadly loaded Jake into the trailer as tears rolled down my cheeks. My best friend and teacher was moving away.

I still remember the sparkle in Cameron's eyes when he first sat on Jake. Over the next 4 years, Jake taught him the same lessons he taught me, and Cameron loved him as much as I did. That's when Jake taught me his last lesson—how to share.   ⋂

Rusty Outsmarted Himself

By Lorna Wityk, Calgary, Alberta

My father had a horse named "Rusty" that was a real con artist. When Dad was riding Rusty, he'd sometimes fake a limp. Thinking Rusty was lame, Dad would turn him out into the pasture to rest and recuperate.

Dad started to get a little suspicious one day when Rusty's lame leg healed miraculously fast. Shortly after he turned him out in the pasture, Dad caught him frolicking and running like nothing was wrong!

Rusty could also be moody. If he was in a good mood, he didn't mind being ridden. However, if he didn't feel like it, he'd walk with such a jarring gait that it would rattle your teeth.

Other times, he'd resort to his fake limp. The fact that Rusty was faking lameness became very clear the day that Dad turned Rusty for home and he suddenly stopped limping. When Dad turned back in the opposite direction and Rusty thought he wasn't going back to the barn, he started limping again…and when Dad headed him home again, he stopped.

The con game was finally up. But that didn't stop Rusty from being one of Dad's favorite horses.

'I Married Bob to Get My Horse Back'

By Irene Stoderl, Melbourne, Florida

I grew up on a ranch in Wyoming, 50 miles from the closest town. Times were tough during the 1930s and '40s, and my parents and I worked hard to make ends meet during the Depression and drought years.

While Dad worked for other ranchers breaking horses and shearing sheep, Mom and I would milk cows, feed orphan lambs and raise chickens and turkeys. We traded eggs for groceries and sold cream, butter, turkeys and fryer chickens to people in town.

Sometimes Dad would buy a string of young horses that needed to be broken. He'd take the rough edge off them, and I would train them to neck rein and work cattle. Then we'd sell them.

One time Dad brought home a small Pinto pony, a Shetland-Arabian

HERBIE was a matchmaker. He brought Irene Stoderl and her husband, Bob (bottom), together for almost 42 years of marriage!

cross. The horse had such a sweet disposition, and I fell in love with him right from the start. We named him "Herbie" after the fellow who sold him to Dad.

After we worked with Herbie all spring, I was so unhappy when Dad sold him to a young man named Bob, who worked for his father lambing and shearing sheep. I didn't know him and was concerned Dad had sold Herbie to someone who wouldn't love and care for him as I had.

I got to know Bob when I started high school. Bob's family lived near town, and since I lived so far out in the country, I roomed and boarded there to begin my freshman year.

After my 4 years of high school and Bob's 3-year tour with the Air Force during World War II, we met again. To my surprise, he still had Herbie! We got married, and three of our four children learned to ride on that lovable horse.

I believe it was God's plan for Dad to sell Herbie to Bob. It led me to find a good and faithful husband for almost 42 years. ∩

Hang on! This Horse Could Really Fly

By Eugene Barker, American Fork, Utah

Growing up on the farm near Fairview, Utah in the 1930s, I had a special horse named "Fly".

She was a saddle horse, but she also filled in when another draft horse was needed in the field. We also used her to herd cattle and pull a cart when we went to town. I rode her many miles to and from school.

We called her Fly because she was quick and fast. In fact, when you mounted her, you'd better be prepared to go or she'd take off without you!

EUGENE BARKER rode Fly many miles to and from school.

That was especially true if we were heading home. I could drop the reins on her neck, turn her loose and she wouldn't stop running until she got to the barn.

One summer, my brother went to work in the coal mines at Schofield, about 30 miles across the mountains from our place. He rode Fly and sent her running home after he got there.

This time, however, Fly did not make it home, and we thought we'd lost her. But in the fall, she showed up at our farm. We found out later that a couple cowboys had caught her as she was crossing the mountains and rode her all summer to herd their cattle.

Once, a man came to the farm to do some mechanical work. When it was time for him to go home, Dad suggested

> "*The last we saw, the mechanic had both arms around Fly's neck, and she was running full speed...*"

he ride Fly rather than walk the 3 miles to town. Dad assured him that Fly could find her way back to the farm by herself.

Dad also cautioned the fellow not to make any quick moves after he mounted—and not to kick her sides. But when he got on, he turned to wave to us and accidentally touched Fly's side. Off she went!

The last we saw of them, the mechanic had both arms wrapped around her neck, and she was running full speed toward town. We assumed he made it to town okay, for Fly soon came home alone. We all had a good laugh over it.

Fly played a big part in our recreation, too. We used her to pull the children on their sleighs and to take us to the hills to ski.

When I rode to school in the wintertime, I would sometimes take my skis with me. After school, I'd tie my lariat to the saddle horn, put on my skis and hold on tight as Fly pulled me home.

I'd get dumped once in a while. But good ol' Fly would stop and wait for me to pick myself up.

How I wish I could have one more ride on her. ∩

Tinkerbell Was Sweet on Sugar

By Peg Stephens, Lapeer, Michigan

When we moved to Clark Lake, Michigan, there was a pony shed attached to our garage. So it wasn't long before our two German shepherd dogs, black cat and a white rabbit named "Sugar" were joined by a Shetland pony, "Tinkerbell".

When winter came, we decided to put Sugar's cage in the pony shed with Tinkerbell. That way the pony's body heat could keep the rabbit warm.

Somehow, Sugar kept getting out of her cage. We couldn't figure it out because we always stuck a stick into the latch to keep the door closed, and there was no way she could reach it from inside the cage.

Spring came and the mystery continued—Sugar kept getting out of her cage. We noticed, too, that Sugar and Tinkerbell were becoming inseparable. We'd find them grazing nose to nose…or if Tinkerbell would stretch out on the ground, so would Sugar.

Then one day we discovered how Sugar was getting out. We caught Tinkerbell nudging the stick out of the latch of the cage with her nose to free her buddy. Mystery solved!

Kendra Bond

JUST LIKE TINKERBELL, this horse seemed to be a barnyard favorite with other animals.

BONNIE PAULIN gave Cash lots of TLC, and eventually she won over his heart—and vice versa.

Ornery Horse Responded to Love

By Bonnie Paulin, Decatur, Alabama

I'll never forget the day I bought a 3-year-old Quarter Horse named "Cash".

Money was tight, but it had been 5 years since I owned a horse. So I wanted one badly and was able to work out a deal with Cash's previous owner.

The first time I mounted Cash, before he even took a step, he jumped up on all fours. When he landed, he slipped in the mud and onto his belly. I supposed the smart thing to do would have been to call off the deal right then and there, but I didn't. Like a fool, I gave Cash another chance, and to this day, I'm glad for that "foolish" decision.

I had ridden all of my life and considered myself to have a good seat in the saddle. But Cash could be a stinker and threw me every chance he had. To make matters worse, I think he had a smile on his face every time he did!

But I was just as stubborn as that little bay. I gave him lots of tender loving care despite how much I wanted to "have it out with him" when he had his temper tantrums. I trusted God to make us best friends.

Finally, after 6 months of bumps and bruises from being thrown, Cash responded to my love and we became a team. We spent years competing at horse shows and just having fun swimming on the beach.

Cash became so gentle that a 10-year-old rode him in a jump competition…and a 66-year-old woman took hunt seat lessons on him.

After our bruising start, Cash became priceless to me.　◯

Daisy Was Grateful

By Harriet Francis, Bethany, Oklahoma

W hen we were living in the mountains of Kentucky in the 1930s, we had a dark colored little mare named "Daisy". How I loved her.

We spent hours riding up and down the mountain trails and through the waters of the creek beds along the way.

One day it was freezing cold as we were crossing the creek to get home. When we arrived, my parents had a large pail of warm salt water and a cloth waiting. I bathed Daisy's legs one by one in the warm water to wash off the ice clinging to them and to prevent them from getting sore.

I'll never forget Daisy's neigh when I finished. It was as if she was saying "thank you".

I led her into her stall and gave her some corn. Only then did I go to the house for my supper of corn bread.　◯

She Had an Old Army Saddle—
And a Gunnysack for a Blanket

By Cathryn Driskel, Lees Summit, Missouri

One June morning in the 1940s, my father woke me to tell me we had a new colt. He took me behind the barn, where our old workhorse, "Dolly", had given birth to the prettiest sorrel foal.

She had a white mane, and her tail was white and sorrel striped. It was wavy, too, just like she had been to the beauty parlor. I named her "June" and spent every spare moment with her.

When June got older, Dad helped me break her to ride. Since she was half workhorse and half saddle horse, she was bigger than most horses and a challenge to mount, especially since I didn't have a saddle. I climbed on by wrapping my toes around her leg.

The neighbor kids had real saddle horses, and I was sometimes ashamed that I didn't have a fancy saddle, bridle or even a pretty saddle blanket for June. Sometimes I'd paint June's bit silver. But it only lasted until she started to slobber.

However, my big clumsy horse could run just as fast as the other horses. So we had a good time riding all over the countryside on Sunday afternoons with my friends.

One day a neighbor gave me an old Army saddle. I found a gunnysack for a blanket and proudly saddled June. We must have looked quite a sight. But the saddle kept my bottom dry when I rode and made it easier to mount and dismount in ladylike fashion.

June gave us two colts. They followed at a distance when I rode June. I learned to nicker like their mother, and when I did, the colts would hurry to catch up to us. I'd tie them to June's tail when we rode near the main highway. What a picture that was, but I didn't care.

One summer night I rode June to school for band practice. I tied her carefully to a big post outside the school, but when it was time to go home, she wasn't there. I was frightened because if she had decided to go home without me, she would have had to cross the busy highway.

But before I could panic, June came up to me. Someone had untied her, but she loved me as much as I loved her and wasn't about to leave without me. ∩

Little Horse Had a Big Heart

By Layne Ment, Lethbridge, Alberta

I've raised and trained horses all my life, and I've known some good ones. But the one that really stands out is "Dexter".

I spotted Dexter at a sale. I don't normally buy horses that way, but there was something special about him. He was put up for sale because he was too small and light to be a roping horse. He was a half inch under 15 hands and weighed 1,050 pounds. But to me, he was the biggest horse in the world.

Dexter was 5 when I got him, and we were together until he was 12. During that time, he won the Alberta Heavyweight Competitive Trail Ride and Best Conditioned Horse Award twice.

More importantly, he was my best friend—closer to me than most people. I know that when I go to Heaven, I'll find Dexter peacefully grazing on God's ranch. ∩

A LITTLE HORSE named Dexter stood out among all the horses Layne Ment has trained.

BEVERLY WILLIAMS shared a can of Pepsi with Apache in this old photo from the family album.

He Had a 'Bottled Up' Craving

By Beverly Williams, Blanchester, Ohio

Once I had a black and white Paint named "Apache" that loved to drink out of a bottle. Red soda pop was his favorite, and since his face was white, the pop gave him beautiful pink lips!

We owned a dairy back in the days when the milk was put in glass bottles. One day we heard the sound of breaking glass. We looked out to see Apache next to a case of milk bottles waiting to be filled. One by one, he was pulling them out of a case. When he discovered they were empty, he dropped them crashing to the cement. ∩

She Learned to Crochet While Riding Prince

By Dorothy Freeman, Oakton, Virginia

Back in 1930, when I was 10, my family moved from a small Kansas town to my grandfather's farm. In spite of the drought, dust and lack of electricity and indoor plumbing, I truly loved farm life.

One of my fondest memories is of "Prince", a saddle horse my father purchased for me to herd the milk cows. We didn't have a lot of fences, and it was my job to take the cows to grass and keep them from straying while they grazed.

Prince and I spent many hours riding all over the farm, usually with me singing at the top of my lungs for the sheer joy of the freedom I felt.

Then Daddy bought a young herd bull to run with the cows. The bull had a mean streak, so I had strict instructions not to dismount Prince while I was tending to the cattle.

This really wasn't a hardship, because my big Western saddle was comfortable, and Prince was a very patient horse. To pass the time, I looped a leg over the saddle horn, pulled a book out of my overalls pocket and read while the cows grazed.

One day, however, I became completely engrossed in my book. When I finally looked up, the cows had strayed across the road into the yard of the country school. I was frantically trying to round them up when my father came by. Together, we got the cows back where they belonged. But after that, Daddy wouldn't allow me to read on the job!

Since I was spending so many hours herding cows and helping with the farm chores, Mother decided I needed to work on developing some feminine skills, too. Oh, woe!

She and I embroidered a doily together, then she began teaching me to crochet an edge to go around it. I took the doily, thread and crochet hooks with me every time Prince and I herded cows. But I didn't have trouble keeping my eyes on the cows because I enjoyed reading a lot more than I liked to crochet!

I still have that doily—with the crocheted edge finally completed. When I show my handiwork to my grandchildren, they find it difficult to believe I did it while riding Prince and herding the cows.

Gentle Horse Was a Lifesaver In a Blizzard

By Dale Williamson, Lakeland, Florida

My favorite horse on the Nebraska farm where I grew up in the 1920s and '30s was a Morgan named "Diamond". He was black with a white diamond-shaped spot on his head.

Diamond could be used to work in the fields, but he was primarily a riding and buggy horse. He was so gentle that we could crawl under his belly and between his legs.

If one or more children sat on his back, he'd walk around slowly and cautiously so they wouldn't fall off. But when a bigger person mounted, he could sure do some prancing. He could be ridden with or without a saddle. We even used him to rope cattle.

We kids played cowboys on him, leaning over his shoulder, pretending to shoot at outlaws from under his neck. We could drop the reins over his head, and he'd remain where he was standing indefinitely. But if we put the reins over the saddle horn and told him to go home, he would do so.

I rode Diamond to school, and my younger brother, Les, rode a Shetland pony named "Pal". While we were in class one afternoon, a snowstorm came roaring in. On our way home, the snowdrifts were so deep that short-legged Pal wasn't able

DIAMOND was so gentle that even Dale Williamson's little brother, Les, could ride him (left). But normally Dale rode Diamond and Les rode a pony named Pal (above).

to get through them.

So I dismounted and threw Diamond's reins over the saddle horn. He plowed a path through each drift and then waited for us to come through. I believe he saved our lives that day.

Old Friends Meet Again

By Roy Hartl, Loyal, Wisconsin

We had a special horse named "Kernel" when I was a kid growing up on a Wisconsin farm.

I remember riding Kernel out to the woods the winter I was in eighth grade. I took my ax along to cut firewood. I'd fell a large tree and hook Kernel up to it. He'd pull it through the brush and head for home, stopping right by the woodpile.

Dad eventually sold Kernel to a man who lived about 40 miles away. About 3 years later, we heard the fellow no longer wanted Kernel, so Dad and I went to bring him home.

After all that time, Kernel remembered us—he walked up to us and laid his head on my shoulder. When we got him home, he went straight to the barn and into his old stall.

Circus Pony Provided a Th

By Vicki Robinson, Murphy, North Carolina

When I was about 10, Daddy bought me a Pinto pony from a carnival that was passing through. His name was "Trig".

Most horses have a tendency to appear sweet-tempered until they see you coming with a bridle and a saddle blanket, then they turn tail and run. Not my Trig. He would let me saddle him, bridle him, put ribbons in his tail and a bonnet on his head. He was truly a gentle and forgiving animal—except once.

It was a typical summer day, hot and long. Having driven my mama crazy, I decided I'd go play with Trig and drive him crazy for a while. I crawled on Trig, laid back and started to doze. He continued to graze contentedly. Neither of us had a care in the world.

There was an old hound dog in the next pasture that acted like he owned the whole countryside. Trig and I always steered clear of that place. But on that particular day, the dog found a hole in the fence.

The dog's baying woke me from my snooze, and the next thing I knew, he was heading straight for Trig and me. Trig started kicking the hound and then took off at a full gallop. In the commotion, I slid under his neck. All I could do to avoid

"All I could do to avoid getting trampled was to wrap my legs around his neck and hang onto his ears…"

getting trampled was to wrap my legs around his neck and hang onto his ears.

Poor Trig, bless his heart, was getting it from both ends—a dog nipping at his heels and a squealing youngster hanging onto his ears. I can only imagine the options going through his mind—like kicking higher to get the dog or heading for the pond to drown the kid.

Fortunately for me, Trig ran for the barn instead of the

132

pond. At one point, I remember looking up and seeing his lips move. To this day, I wonder if he was mumbling something about this kid hanging on for dear life or whether he was trying to comfort me.

With the barn in sight, Trig slowed down just long enough to send a kick that scared the hound away. Once he got to the barn, which seemed like a million miles away, he gently lowered me to the ground.

Then, without as much as a whinny or a flip of the tail, he headed back to the pasture to make sure that hound was gone for good.

I went straight to the house, wondering whether I should tell Mama about my adventure. Nope—I decided not to. She probably wouldn't have believed a horse tale like that any-way...and if she did, I'd have really been in trouble.

Thanks for the Laughs and Memories

By Marianne French Hammond, Hillsborough, New Hampshire

Hilltoppins was born at the top of a hill on our family farm in New Hampshire.

He was a cute chestnut Morgan colt, a real fun-loving little guy. He'd steal Dad's hat off his head while he was busy working in the yard. We had to ban him from the kitchen, where he tried to beg for carrots and snacks.

His best trick, however, was opening the stall doors in the barn, no matter what kind of contraption we installed to lock them. Many times, I'd wake up to the sound of hoofbeats in the night after he'd let his mother, his sister and all the other horses out of their stalls.

Thank you, Hilltoppins, for all the laughs and memories you gave us.

THIS BEAUTY was born on Marianne Hammond's birthday. She grew up with horses.

He Bucked at the Drop of a Hat

By Lisa Buchanan, Herrick, Illinois

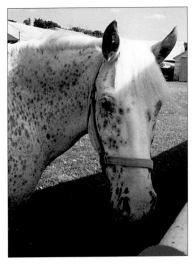

TOMAHAWK gave his owner, Lisa Buchanan, a few embarrassing moments. But it was worth it.

My parents gave me a beautiful 3-year-old Appaloosa gelding named "Tomahawk" for my 12th birthday.

That was more than 20 years ago, but I will never forget the night Dad brought him home. I was already in my nightgown when Dad asked me if I would like to see my birthday surprise.

None of us realized then what a special bond of friendship would blossom between Tomahawk and me. All I knew that night was my parents had made me the happiest girl in the world as I went out to the barn lot and saw Tomahawk standing there.

I loved riding Tomahawk in parades along with Dad. In fact, I rode in one area parade for 17 consecutive years.

At our local parade one Fourth of July, I dropped my hat right in front of Tomahawk. That startled him and he started bucking. I just barely managed to stay in the saddle and was teased about Tomahawk bucking "at the drop of a hat".

Tomahawk really was a very mild-mannered horse, even if he threw me more than any other horse I have ever ridden. He was green-broke when we bought him and was not fond of the saddle, which was the cause of a few of the dumps.

I also fell off one time when he was startled by several birds fluttering out of the trees where we were riding. He came back to me as I was sprawled on the ground, a little dazed, and stood there waiting until I could mount up to go home.

I rode Tomahawk to school a few times and tied him behind the shop classroom. I remember sitting in English class one day and looking out the window to see him grazing on the baseball field. I raised my hand to ask the teacher if I could go catch him. She very calmly replied, "Yes, Lisa, I think you should."

I can still feel the eyes of the whole school watching me as I ran around the diamond after him.　　　　　　　　⋂

Sleigh Bells Made Him Prance

By George Curtis, Payson, Utah

I bought "Blackie" as a yearling colt. Actually, I traded a ton of hay for him to a fellow who was running low on feed.

He was a small and shaggy desert mustang, and we had him for 3 years before we broke him to ride. Then my four sons began riding him daily and he became gentle as a kitten.

Blackie was so smart that he could turn on the lights in the barn and the water in the trough. Problem is, he never turned them off! He also loved to hear sleigh bells. He would really prance to make them ring.

Blackie got loose once while I was up in the mountains camping with friends. They joked that it would be a long walk home if I had to carry Blackie's saddle. But as soon as we started the breakfast fire and the smoke filtered through the trees, he came back to camp. Guess he figured it was time for his breakfast, too. ⋂

BLACKIE was a wild mustang that became so gentle even children could ride him.

Sickly Colt Grew Up to Be A Very Special Horse

By Mary Niles, Street, Maryland

JESSIE is a calm and patient mount for his Special Olympics riders.

Jessie James was a "nothing special" horse born in someone's backyard almost 20 years ago. I was a typical, horse-crazy young girl when I answered an ad in the local newspaper that read: "5-month-old buckskin Quarter Horse colt for sale." I paid $100 for him.

I was, and still am, lucky to live near my grandfather's picturesque farm just outside Bel Air, Maryland. My grandfather let me bring Jessie home to the farm and raise him—along with my orphaned calf, "Maggie", and a shepherd-mix pup named "Ponch" I found abandoned in the woods.

Jessie grew from a scrawny sickly foal with a dull brown coat into a healthy handsome horse with a slick, deep-golden coat and a shiny black mane and tail. As I began training him, I soon discovered how smart and willing to please he was. One day I was leading him around with a rope, and before I knew it, I was on his back riding him.

He really showed me his calm and level-headed temperament the day I found him trapped in a tangled mess of old barbed wire in a meadow. He didn't move a muscle as I cut the wire away, and he escaped with only minor cuts and scratches.

136

As time went on, I discovered Jessie had more talents—the patience, intuition and gentleness to be a therapeutic riding horse for people with special needs. So we got involved in a program that gives these people the chance to learn the joy of riding. Jessie soon became the favorite among all the children who visited the farm.

"Country Boy" at Home in City

What amazed me was the smooth way Jessie handled all the new environments in which he was put. Here was a "country boy" that hadn't left the farm from the day he arrived as a colt. Now, we were taking him to fund-raising events and horse shows for special needs riders and making a yearly trip to the city for the Special Olympics.

At the Special Olympics, he finds himself in the middle of a busy college campus just outside Baltimore with loud speakers, buses and crowds of people. In spite of the commotion, Jessie remains calm and steady—his beautiful coat shining as brightly as the gold medals his proud young riders win.

Freckles Didn't Like to Go To School

By Dorothea Hinton
Brule, Nebraska

FRECKLES would rear up to remind his rider he didn't like to leave home.

I am 86 years old and could go on and on about the wonderful life I had growing up on a farm.

I was the youngest of eight children, 10 years younger than my youngest brother. We raised a few cattle, lots of hogs, turkeys and chickens. We milked cows twice a day and bucket-fed the baby calves.

But the thing I remember most was a horse named "Freckles". He was the horse I rode to school. He didn't like to leave home, so every morning he'd rear up a couple of times to remind me of this. But he'd eventually settle down and go.

The school was about 7 miles from home. It was built of sod and had an old potbellied stove for heat.

Some winters, the snow was so deep and drifted that I could ride right over the fences. I liked that because I didn't have to stop and open the gates. But I did have to wear lots of heavy clothes, which made it difficult to climb on.   ∩

They Got Some Religion After The Donkey Roundup

By Ginger Lyons, Elizabethton, Tennessee

I must have been about 11 years old when I first met "Pearl". She was a white Quarter Horse with dappled spots of black and brown across her hips and belonged to my neighbor Johnny.

Johnny and I became best friends because I was constantly at his place to visit his horse. I'd help him with chores to earn the privilege of a ride.

The farm in northeast Tennessee where Johnny lived had large patches of woods and was hilly and full of rocks. Goats loved the place and must have given Pearl tips on how to run up and down the steep terrain.

There was also a pair of donkeys on the farm that tried to escape from the barnyard whenever Johnny and I opened the gate to get Pearl for a ride. I think they'd see us coming and immediately plan their escape.

One of the donkeys was calm and easy to retrieve. But the other was not so friendly. He'd bite and even chase us into the woods when we went after him.

One day when this donkey with an attitude got loose, Johnny and I decided we'd become cowboys to get him back. We knew where he was hiding out in the woods (the goofy crit-

138

ter always went to the same place). So Johnny grabbed a rope and we took off riding double.

In our haste, we didn't put the saddle on Pearl, just the bridle. But with our plan laid out, we rode up and down several hills, across the creek, under branches and around thorny bushes to where we knew the donkey was hiding.

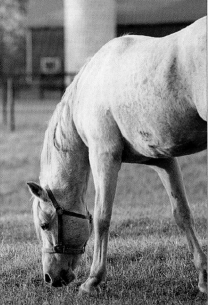
Bob Firth/Firth PhotoBank

Johnny made a large lasso with the rope as he approached the donkey on foot. The plan was for me to come up from behind on Pearl and keep the ornery critter from retreating in that direction. Sounded easy.

Just as Johnny threw the rope, he stepped in a rabbit hole. The rope hit its mark around the donkey's beefy neck, but down went Johnny. He dropped the rope and the donkey took off, braying as he ran out of sight.

Pearl Had a Plan

When the donkey started running, Pearl took off after him—with me hanging on for dear life. I tried to stop her, but she had a plan of action, and I couldn't change her mind.

My legs were holding on so tight I thought my eyeballs were going to pop out. I was getting hit by tree limbs and was afraid to look up. But I did see the donkey running up a very steep trail, and it was evident Pearl was going to follow.

Right in the middle of that hill, my strength gave out. I did a backward somersault off Pearl and didn't stop going end over end until I reached the bottom. By this time, Johnny was standing over me laughing. I was laughing just as hard.

Pearl chased that donkey all the way home. We gave her the best brushing and her favorite treat for all of her hard work.

As for Johnny and me, we spent the rest of the day practicing our verses for Bible school. We figured it was much safer than playing cowboys and rounding up donkeys. ∩

'I'd Be Mad If My Grandkids Tried Half the Tricks I Did!'

By Ruby Rayburn, Columbia, Mississippi

The great thing about growing up on a farm was that I was never without pets. I had dogs, cats, calves, turtles, rabbits, squirrels and a goat. But of all the animals on the farm, the one I loved most was my horse "Twankie".

Twankie was a large chestnut gelding and my best friend, since my closest neighbors lived a half mile away. His mother was my dad's first horse, a mustang from Texas. His sire was a plow horse. Twankie got his mother's color and his father's size.

In spite of his parentage, Twankie was as beautiful as a Thoroughbred to me…and he was as versatile as a Morgan when it came to working, riding and performing. He had a well-proportioned head with wide-spaced eyes and a small star on his forehead. His broad back offered a comfortable seat and assurance for youngsters like me just learning to ride.

Twankie was intelligent, usually patient and occasionally mischievous, but never mean. He could open the corncrib door and gates but was smart enough to not overeat or get into danger by leaving the pasture. In short, Twankie was the ideal pet.

Good thing, because as a child, I didn't know danger. I stood on Twankie's back while he cantered. Because I couldn't climb on him when I was small, I waited until he put his head down to eat grass, then sat on his neck. When he raised his head, I slid down his neck, turned around and rode off.

The most dangerous thing I did was hold his tail, put my feet on his hind legs and climb up his rump. (I should have had a serious spanking for that!) I'd be very upset if my grandchildren did half the tricks I did with Twankie.

Later on, I trained Twankie to lie down. That made it easier to get on him. This trick also came in handy when we played hide-and-seek on horses. It was a lot easier to hide on a horse that will lie down behind bushes!

My parents said I named Twankie when I was small. Only the Lord knows where I got the name. But one thing's for sure—I never felt poor because I owned a treasure of a horse. ○

BEASTY might look fearless, but she was easily frightened until owner Amy North accepted the challenge of training her.

Big Beast Turned Out to Be a Real Beauty

By Amy North, Nashua, New Hampshire

I grew up in central Pennsylvania surrounded by dairy farms. No one bothered to buy me dolls for my birthdays because all I ever wanted was a horse.

But we couldn't own a horse because my brother was extremely allergic to them. The best I could do was play with my toy horse collection, read the entire *Black Stallion* series of books and dream that I would come home someday and find a golden Palomino in the garage.

When I was 9, all those years of begging paid off, and my parents said I could start taking riding lessons. We had to drive nearly 45 minutes to a stable because I wanted to learn to ride English, and most people only rode Western where I lived. I was a little disappointed when I didn't get to ride like the wind the first lesson, but after 3 years of lessons, I was able to join the local 4-H pony club. I was the only one without a horse and the only one who rode English.

Eventually I did get the horse of my dreams, a huge, high-spirited 3-year-old bay Thoroughbred. She was tall and elegant and looked as if she could leap the moon. I believed I could tame this huge beast, which soon became her affectionate name.

Much to my surprise, "Beasty" had not been taught many things before I got her. The first time I tried to pick her feet, I ended up scraping myself off the wall!

She was afraid of an open field and would cower near the barn. She didn't know she could drink from the stream, so she'd come into the barn at night and thirstily drink three

> *"The first time I tried to pick her feet, I ended up scraping myself off the wall..."*

buckets of water. She knew how to run but didn't understand that I wanted her to stop without flying over her head like a launched missile.

Despite the difficulties, I was up for the challenge. The fact that Beasty was petrified of an open field opened up some opportunities for us to become closer—she was always grateful to see me. Eventually I even was able to lead her to a stream and get her to drink, disproving the old adage.

Beasty's first horse show was very frightening for her. But one of the instructors was so impressed by her potential that she offered to give us lessons. We did great at the next show, and with the instructor's continued help, Beasty and I finally started to connect with each other. Only 9 months later, we won seventh place at the state horse show.

I've had Beasty for 16 years now. I know that someday I'll have to say good-bye—until we get to ride again in the endless fields of Heaven. ∩

The Horse Knew the Way...

By Lorri Bisconer, Battle Ground, Washington

I could tell hundreds of stories about the many experiences I had with my buckskin mare, "Tammy". But the most memorable is one I have kept a secret for 20 years.

My cousin, Spence, was a cattleman who had ranches near Lyle and Trout Lake, Washington and a 10,000-acre cattle grazing allotment in the Gifford Pinchot National Forest. Every spring, we would drive the cattle from his Lyle ranch across country up into the mountains.

In the fall, we would spend a week or so rounding up the cattle and driving them out of the mountains down to the Trout Lake ranch. The cattle would stay there until about January 1, when we would drive them to Lyle, where they finished the winter. In spring, we did it all over again.

One fall on the way out of the forest, Spence became concerned about a bunch of cows that were missing. He found their tracks and decided to set out after them. But he wanted the rest of us to keep the main herd moving. He told me to take the point and keep the herd headed in the right direction, while the rest of the crew brought up the rear and kept the cattle from scattering.

LORRI BISCONER confidently rides Tammy, her faithful buckskin that kept a 20-year secret.

I was terrified! I'd been helping the family out on these drives for about 15 years, and I had ridden Tammy for 5 of them. But Spence had always been in the point position.

I didn't have a clue about which way to go. I gave

Tammy a pat on the neck and told her it was going to be up to her to get us through the forest. I made no attempt to guide her, and she headed out like everything was under control. Her ears were pointed straight ahead, and she lowered her head to the ground from time to time to sniff. When we came to a fork in the trail, she would stop, look both ways and then decide which fork to take.

Left the Decisions to Tammy

She did this time after time—stop, sniff and choose. Gradually, I began to recognize a few landmarks along the trail and started to relax.

There were the caves where Spence told me settlers stored their butter to keep it from spoiling in the summer. Then came the old homestead where we always met at the end of summer for a big family picnic with homemade ice cream and three-legged sack races. There was the creek where we watered the herd. It was coming back to me. Still, I left all the decisions to Tammy.

It was about 8 miles out of the mountains down to the main highway—the most nerve-racking miles I have ever ridden. By the time we reached the bottom, Spence and his wayward cows had caught up with us, and everyone was praising the job I had done.

Of course, I showed great humility in accepting their praise. "Oh, it was nothing," I assured them. But that night, Tammy got an extra helping of grain, a bigger pile of hay and a lot of TLC from her very grateful friend.   ◯

Houdini of the Horse Barn

By Kathryn Winkler, Fairfax, Virginia

The most wonderful horse our family has ever owned is "Wadsworth", a Quarter Horse and Welsh pony cross. It was love at first sight when we met this 10-year-old liver-colored chestnut with a blaze face and four white socks.

Wads loves to eat different foods, including blackberries. Often over the years, I would go out into the pasture and call him. He'd come galloping from the backside of the acreage, neighing the entire time. As he came near, I could see his snowy white blaze was blue from all the wild blackberries he had eaten. He looked like a kid with his hand in the cookie jar.

Wads also enjoys Oreo cookies and pizza. He likes 7-Up, too, but his favorite drink is Orange Crush!

Wadsworth is a regular Houdini that can open deadbolt locks. I tried to warn our friend Maria when she borrowed

> *"Not only had Wadsworth let himself out of his stall, but he let out three other horses as well!"*

Wads for her daughter to show. But she said not to worry—she was experienced working with horses that thought they could outwit humans.

The barn Maria put Wads in had seven stalls around a large open riding arena. She called me the morning after she picked him up to tell me that when she went to feed the horses, she heard thuds, grunts, snorts and whinnies coming from the barn. As she opened the door, there were four horses in the arena playing tag. Not only had Wads let himself out of his stall, but he had let out three other horses as well!

I explained to Maria how Wads got out because I'd watched him do it before. He delicately takes the deadbolt in his teeth, with his eyes almost shut, like he was a burglar listening to the tumblers as he picked a lock. Then he slides the deadbolt back. Next he works his nose between the stall door and door frame and slides the door open.

Houdini couldn't do it any better! ∩

WADSWORTH is a willing ride-giver to Kathryn Winkler's grandchildren, Brooke, 7-1/2 months, Kiley, 9, and Brett Lyles, 5.

Mother Was Surprised When the Horse Walked into the Living Room

By Evelyn Pacha, Atkinson, Nebraska

When our son Cliff was 5 years old, we surprised him with a beautiful little spotted filly named "Tootsie". She was a typical young Shetland full of tricks, and Cliff always rode her bareback.

I can still picture Tootsie standing patiently outside the kitchen door waiting for some crackers or maybe a carrot or apple. Many times Cliff would hold the door open so she could come on in. If there was any food on the table, she'd clean it up, but she wasn't too careful about the dishes.

One time, my mischievous father opened the door when my mother was entertaining ladies of her club in the living room. The ladies were more than a little startled to hear Tootsie clomping over the hardwood floors into the living room to beg for treats.

We named Tootsie's first colt "Mickey". The kids trained them both to roll over when they clapped their hands.

Many times, the two horses rode in the backseat of our Chevy. Once, we came across a family with a flat tire. When we stopped to help, our children opened the car door and out jumped the little horses.

The other family could not believe their eyes. Mickey and Tootsie gave them rides while we waited for the tire to be changed.

EVELYN PACHA shared this photo of her children with Tootsie and her first colt, Mickey.

147

Ruby Was a Good Horse— If You Played by Her Rules

By Frances Garber, Harrisonburg, Virginia

When I was 11 years old, I passed the county tests given to seventh graders to be promoted to high school.

To get to the high school, I had to ride a horse. I took Dad's workhorse for the first 2 weeks of school. But then Dad needed the horse to work his ground for fall seeding. It was time to do some serious horse hunting.

Dad found a white five-gaited Kentucky saddle horse named "Ruby". Her owner told Dad that she could be mean-spirited if you did not follow her rules.

She'd kick if you went into her stall on her right side. However, if you called out her name and went in on the left, she minded her manners.

Her owner also told Dad that we would never be able to catch Ruby in the field. But he assured us that after she was with us a month or two, Ruby could be trusted to come home if she broke loose.

When our neighbor came down to see my new horse and heard what the owner had told my dad, he was afraid for me to ride her. But I felt very grown up when Daddy said, "She can handle her."

I never had any problems as long as I obeyed Ruby's rules. Later, I was even able to catch her in an open field by holding her bridle behind me and walking toward her eating an apple. She always came to me.

After Christmas, my cousins wanted me to spend the night with them so I could see their new Christmas present, a wonderful battery-powered radio. However, they didn't have a stable for Ruby for the night. When I mentioned it to Dad, he said, "This will be a good time to see if Ruby will really come home by herself."

So on Monday morning, I rode Ruby most of the way to the schoolhouse, gathered my lunch box and book satchel and turned Ruby around to send her home. She was reluctant and wanted to go on to her stall at school. But when I smacked her on the rump and clapped my hands, she headed down the road in her fox-trot gait.

I thought about Ruby all day and wished the school had a telephone so I could call home to see if she had made it. As soon as I arrived at my cousins' house after school, I did call and was relieved to find out she found her way home okay.

A couple mornings later on my way to school, Mr. Akers came running out of his sawmill with his hands up. "Wait a

> "*When* a man reached for her bridle, Ruby reared up, pawed at him high in the air and ran away…"

minute," he said. "I was so worried about how you'd get home the other day when I saw your horse coming down the road without you.

"I told my two men to help me catch her. One man ran toward her and reached for her bridle rein. But Ruby reared up, pawed at him high in the air and ran by him. The other man came up behind her, trying to drive her toward me. She kicked and galloped down the road."

I discovered three men on horses and a man driving a cattle truck had also tried to catch Ruby as she was heading home that day. But she managed to kick and scare their horses and edge the truck right off the road.

They just didn't know about playing by Ruby's rules!

Loving a Horse Is One of Life's Greatest Pleasures

By Karen Biehle, Marietta, Georgia

My Grandpa Hedrick owned and showed horses and so did my cousins. I rode their horses when I visited.

At home, I read every horse book I could find and rode imaginary horses. Even my Barbie dolls rode horses. But it

KAREN BIEHLE is pictured in 1970 riding Missouri's Lucky Lad (above). They rode together on many trail rides, 4-H events, parades and fairs. It was a proud moment when Lad was named Reserve Grand Champion in 1973 (left).

just wasn't the same as having my own horse.

One fall evening, my dad suggested we take a drive. We went out into the country to a farm, where the most beautiful horse I had ever seen stood in the paddock. His name was "Missouri's Lucky Lad", and he was a 3-year-old sorrel gelding with a half moon on his forehead and one white stocking.

Dad asked me if I would like to ride him. I was thrilled.

While I rode, I noticed Dad speaking with the owner, and the next thing I knew, they were asking me if I would like to keep him. I was speechless and couldn't wait until he was delivered to a pasture near our home.

My father's $150 investment that day repaid itself many times over in fun and the responsibility I learned to assume. We began working with a riding instructor, who taught Lad

---

"My father's investment repaid itself many times over in fun and the responsibility I learned..."

---

and me how to ride and show. Every afternoon I took care of him, cleaning his stall, grooming, feeding and loving him.

I joined the 4-H horse program and participated in trail rides, horse shows, parades, demonstrations and youth fairs. Some of my lifelong friendships started through Lad and 4-H.

The following spring, I began showing Lad, and we started winning! At my third horse show, we won first place over a ring full of professional show horses. I was never so happy and proud as I was that night. I still display that trophy on my fireplace mantel.

My last memorable visit with Lad was when I was pregnant with my first daughter. We went on a very short ride, and it was that day I realized I was closing one chapter in my life and starting a new one of parenthood.

So my parents sold Lad to someone who promised to take good care of him. I was glad I was not around that day.

Now, my love for horses has come back greater than ever. My youngest daughter, Heather, who's 9, loves them just as much as I do, and we've found an organization in North Georgia that buys and rehabilitates abused and neglected horses. We volunteer our help to care for the organization's 36 horses and take occasional trail rides.

Recently, my 13-year-old daughter became smitten, too. So I'm trying to convince my husband that it's time to get horses of our own—for I believe that those who have never loved a horse have missed out on one of life's greatest pleasures. ◠

Pony Arrived as Promised

By Sharon Ginter, Seven Valleys, Pennsylvania

I was in fifth grade when I developed rheumatic fever and was told I could not run or play for a year. That was about the time Mom and Dad were looking for a new home. They promised to buy a house with a barn so when I was well, I could finally have the pony I had always dreamed of.

They kept their promise. On my birthday a year later, I got off the school bus and there stood "Blaze", only 5 months old and cute as a button.

I taught him to shake "hands" like a dog does with his paw. I dressed him in Dad's clothes, and I rolled his long tail in Mom's curlers to make him beautiful!

When Dad wasn't home, I would take Blaze up to the porch and knock on the door. Mom would let us into the house.

BLAZE was an expert at getting out of his pasture and running around the neighborhood. Once he was gone for 2 days.

Came into the Kitchen for Cookies

One day she had just finished baking a batch of cookies. As Blaze walked past the kitchen table, he bumped it and we nearly lost the cookies. It was a long time before Dad found out.

Blaze was an expert at getting out of his pasture and running around the neighborhood. Once he escaped while we weren't home and was gone for 2 days. Finally, some neighbors 2 miles away called us to come get him. I was relieved to get him home, but pretty upset with him for being so naughty.

One of Blaze's favorite antics was to run full speed under a tree limb to see if he could knock me off. Or he would run downhill and come to a screeching halt at the creek, where I often got a close-up look at the water, if you know what I mean! But Blaze never meant to hurt me. He just thought these tricks were fun.

When I was about 20, our farmhouse burned down, and I had to board Blaze at a stable. But I visited him often and brought him his favorite treat—chocolate cupcakes.

I had Blaze until he was 30. I still smile at the comical times I had with my best friend. I just hope he is behaving himself better in Heaven than he did for me! ☊

Amazing Mustang Lived to Be 45

By Pam Weaver, Aurora, Oregon

My best friend was a buckskin mustang named "Churley". I saved my money and bought him 25 years ago, when I was 14.

My fondest memories are of getting off the school bus and seeing Churley waiting for me at the gate. I always saved part of my sack lunch for him. He especially liked it when I had a bottle of pop for him to guzzle.

PAM WEAVER and her old friend Churley head out for a ride. They were a team for 25 years.

Churley was a big influence on my decision to go to college to become a veterinarian technician.

Churley was 45 years old when I finally lost him. I know the angels in Heaven are now just as busy as I used to be trying to keep the fences mended so Churley can't get out! ☊

Old Pony Knows She's Still Loved

By Rose Brown, Nottingham, Pennsylvania

The day I got my pony "Treebee" is one I still remember. Dad had attended a sale where I thought they only sold cattle. But Treebee was no cow! She was the most wonderful pony I could have wished for.

I was 4 years old, and she was about 8. We became the best

of friends the minute we laid eyes on one another.

Treebee is an Appaloosa-Hackney cross. She has the spots of a leopard Appaloosa, but as she's grown older, she has become almost pure white.

We didn't have a saddle, so I learned to ride her bareback. Later I was given a Western saddle for Christmas. I still have that little child's saddle as well as my beloved Treebee.

When I look at that little mare now, I think back at the endless patience she had with me as I learned to ride her. I rode her all the time.

She moved with me to Canada and to Pennsylvania when I moved there. Even when I outgrew her, I never gave her up.

Treebee is 38 years old and lives at a privately owned farm near my home. She has lost her hearing and the sight in one eye, but when I take my children to visit her, she knows that she is loved.   ∩

This Little Mare Was Heaven-Sent

By Marla Ware, Moline, Kansas

My husband gave me a nice gelding named "Buck" that my stepson had bred and raised. The only problem was that he stood 15-1/2 hands tall, and as an aging baby boomer with a weight problem, I had a hard time mounting ol' Buck.

I finally convinced my husband and stepson to find me a shorter horse. My stepson began a diligent search and after several months, he called one evening to say there was an ad in the local paper for a small mare priced at $450. No other information was given.

He checked her out and called the next evening with a cautious tone in his voice. The mare was broken, and my stepson liked how she rode—her gaits were smooth, not short and choppy. What's more, she was only about 14 hands, if that.

"What's wrong with her?" we asked.

Old Enough to Vote

"Well, she's quick and can turn on a dime," my stepson said. "I thought you might want something a little easier to handle. She's also old enough to vote. On top of that, she's an Appaloosa."

I never had been crazy about Appaloosas. But my husband was becoming enthused about the mare, and the price was right. "Okay, buy her," I said.

The little mare's name was "Dixie", and she turned out to be a gift from Heaven. Dixie could communicate better than any horse I had ever been around. She let you know she wanted her feed in a particular spot by where she nuzzled the trough. She didn't like the first bit I used on her, and when I switched, she immediately quit tossing her head and chewing the bit.

I learned more about caring for horses from her than I had ever learned before. And when I rode her, I could pretend

---

"I learned more about caring for horses from her than I had ever learned before…"

---

for a while that I was a heroic American cowboy instead of an overweight, aging, female baby boomer.

Dixie was an easy keeper, too. Her feet were good and solid, and I never had to shoe her.

We had some great rides together, particularly to the "north 40", a large hill that allowed you to see for miles, even into Oklahoma. I remember one ride in particular. My husband had joined me riding old "Sandy". We made it to the top of the hill and stopped to rest the horses.

In the distance, I could see a train making a hard pull up the Flint Hills headed west for Cowley County. I heard its long low whistle as it approached an intersection. Dixie heard the whistle, too, and pricked her ears to listen. As I sat there, I wondered where she had heard trains before, what she had seen and where she had been. I wondered about the horseman or woman careful enough to teach her manners and how many riders she'd gently carried over the years.

I must admit that I had a few misgivings about this little Appaloosa when I first got her. But I've lived long enough to learn not to be too quick to judge.

In Hebrews 13:2, it's written, "Do not neglect to show hospitality to strangers, for thereby some have entertained angels unawares." During the years Dixie was in my life, I suspect I entertained an angel.

Her Rides Were Comical

By Judy Dorman, Salt Lake City, Utah

During the late 1940s, when I was about 11 years old, my parents bought an acreage next to the Platte River near Littleton, Colorado. After we moved in, some friends gave me a horse named "Rex". My father bought another horse named "Skeeter".

My fondest memories of those days are of going into the pasture to watch Rex and Skeeter graze.

Then I decided it would be fun to read comic books while sitting on Rex. I'd lead him over to a fence, and without a saddle or bridle, I'd crawl onto his back with my comic books. I peacefully read as Rex wandered around the pasture seeking out the best grass.

When Rex decided I had been there long enough, he slowly walked under a low branch on the apple tree and gently brushed me off his back. We spent many lazy summer days that way.

REX took Judy Dorman on many lazy rides.

GOLDIE was 30 years old when this picture was taken in 1998. She died a year later and is buried in her favorite pasture, where she can look out over the farm and keep tabs on her buddies.

Palomino Had a Mind of Her Own

By Louise Kinnaman, Bayard, Nebraska

As a child growing up in North Platte, Nebraska, I had dreamed of owning a horse. I remember asking for one for every birthday and Christmas. Dad's reply was always, "Where do you think you're going to keep it—in the garage?"

It wasn't until the spring of my first year of teaching in Fort Morgan, Colorado that I decided it was time to make my dream come true. I found "Goldie", a green-broke, 2-year-old golden Palomino. She really lived up to her name as her coat shown like a new penny in the sunlight.

I had big plans for Goldie that summer because I had taken a job as a horse wrangler at a youth camp in the Rocky Mountains. When we went on trail rides, one wrangler always rode in the front and the other brought up the rear. Goldie and I were in the rear.

Not Camera Shy

This gave me the opportunity to take in the spectacular scenery and take some fantastic pictures. Goldie even learned to stand still and pose when I stopped to take her picture. But as soon as she heard the click of the camera, she was ready to start down the trail again. I never got a chance to take a second shot.

There were a lot of "just for fun" horse shows in our area that Goldie and I went to over the years. She performed the best in the trail classes. When maneuvering over an obstacle, she was very careful where she placed each foot so as not to knock it over. She contemplated each move with care and never rushed.

After a while, however, Goldie began to get bored with horse shows and developed a real stubborn streak. She would go through the obstacle course just fine until we got to the bridge. That's when she would balk and refuse to cross.

After the competition, I'd take her back into the arena just to see what she would do and, of course, she would cross the bridge without hesitation. She knew exactly when we were

"Goldie had an amusing habit that scared people who didn't know her..."

being judged and when we weren't. I finally realized she was trying to tell me something, so we quit competing in horse shows.

Goldie had an amusing habit that often scared people who did not know her. She'd walk up to people in the pasture or corral to greet them. But the minute they'd try to scratch her on the head, she would turn her rump to them.

Folks were afraid Goldie was going to kick them. What they didn't realize was that her rump was her favorite place to be scratched. All Goldie was doing was giving them a none-too-subtle hint!

Susie Spread a Lot of Joy

By Barb Wirkus, Malone, Wisconsin

David R. Stoecklein

There wasn't a happier 16-year-old girl alive the day I bought a black and white Paint mare named "Susie". My dad snapped a picture of that proud moment that I still keep on my mantel.

I had taken riding lessons since I was a little kid, longing for the day when I would be able to own my own horse. My parents were very supportive of my dream, but with four other children, they could not afford to buy me a horse.

So I baby-sat, and when I was old enough, I got a job as a kitchen helper at a nursing home. I saved every dime until I finally had enough to buy my beloved Susie. She was a sweet mare, small but sturdy. As a bonus, Susie was pregnant and due to foal in the spring.

Loved to Swim

The stable where I boarded her was near a lake, so we went swimming. She loved it!

There were lots of kids my age who also kept their horses at the stable, so we never lacked for company on our trail rides. I remember packing picnic lunches behind our saddles and spending the entire day on horseback. What wonderful memories Susie and I shared.

I rode her all that autumn and as much as the weather would allow during the cold Wisconsin winter. I loved cantering her through snowdrifts that reached past her knees.

As spring approached, we had to cut our rides short since Susie was getting close to her foaling time. On May 25, 1971, she gave birth to a bright bay stud colt. I named him "Crackerjack". Now I was the owner of not one but two horses.

It wasn't easy, but I managed to support both of them while working and going to college. One of my proudest moments

159

was when Crackerjack won first place in a halter class at a local horse show.

I continued to ride Susie and train Crackerjack whenever I could. But as Crackerjack approached his second birthday, I realized I couldn't do justice to training him. I simply didn't have the time or the experience to teach a horse to wear a saddle and carry a rider. So I made the heartbreaking decision to sell him.

But I still had Susie—at least until I got married. Then I had to make another heartbreaking decision. A teenage girl, who reminded me a little of myself at that age, bought her. A while later, I saw Susie in a parade with her proud new owner astride her, and I knew I had made the right decision.

After that, I lost track of Susie. I never stopped loving horses, but with family responsibilities, a mortgage and car

---

"They had a special bond with an animal that asked for nothing in return..."

---

payments, it was nearly 20 years before I was able to buy another one. Meanwhile, my love for horses had grown even stronger, and now in my 40s, I'm still riding and showing.

I have a neighbor, Julie, who is active in Free S.P.I.R.I.T. (Special People In Riding Therapy). It's an organization that provides physically and emotionally challenged people the opportunity to ride horses.

About a year ago, I was showing Julie photographs of Susie and Crackerjack and noticed a puzzled look on her face. She kept staring at Susie's picture. "That mare looks like one of our therapy horses," she said. "Her name is Susie, too."

I had to laugh. "Sorry," I told Julie. "My Susie would be way over 30 years old by now. I'm sure she passed away years ago."

Still, Julie looked unconvinced. "I have a picture of our Susie at home. I'll be right back."

She ran home and got the picture. My eyes widened as I placed the recent photo next to the one Dad had taken the day I bought Susie. The markings matched perfectly. In disbelief, I said, "It can't be. She can't still be alive."

"Let's check around," Julie said, and she started making phone calls. She called the girl who was currently taking care of Susie, and from there, she was able to backtrack and discover that, sure enough, Susie was my former horse—my first love.

Susie had never left the area and had not had many owners. Each of them had nice things to say about her. But those who praised her the highest were the people of the Free S.P.I.R.I.T. program—the handicapped, abused and disturbed who had a special bond with an animal that asked for nothing in return. I was so glad they had found Susie…and that Susie had found them.

Flood of Memories

After we made the discovery, Julie took me to see Susie. The memories came flooding back as the little mare walked toward me as she had so often in days long ago.

She walked stiffly, her face was flecked with gray and her back was swayed. Yet, I'd have known her anywhere. My Susie! Tears ran down my face as I held onto her halter, while Julie snapped our picture.

The Free S.P.I.R.I.T. folks told me that Susie passed away last September. She simply did not have the energy to get up anymore. That's all right, Susie. You lived a long life and gave a lot of joy to many people. ∩

Bob Firth/Firth PhotoBank